T0071300

MEDITATION ON PERCEPTION

MEDITATION ON PERCEPTION

TEN HEALING PRACTICES TO CULTIVATE MINDFULNESS

Bhante Gunaratana

Foreword by Bhikkhu Bodhi

Wisdom Publications
199 Elm Street
Somerville, MA 02144 USA
www.wisdomexperience.org

Library of Congress Cataloging-in-Publication Data
Gunaratana, Henepola, 1927– author.
  Meditation on perception : ten healing practices to cultivate mindfulness / Bhante Gunaratana.
    pages cm
  Includes bibliographical references and index.
  ISBN 978-1-61429-085-8 (pbk. : alk. paper) — ISBN 1-61429-085-7 (pbk. : alk. paper) —
ISBN 978-1-61429-105-3 (ebook)
  1. Meditation—Buddhism. 2. Perception. I. Title.
  BQ5612.G855 2014
  294.3'4435—dc23
                                  2013047898
  ISBN 978-1-61429-085-8   ebook ISBN 978-1-61429-105-3

25 24 23 22 21
6   5   4   3

Cover design by Phil Pascuzzo. Interior design by Gopa&Ted2, Inc.
Set in Diacritical Garamond Pro 11.5/16.6.

For more information, please visit www.fscus.org.

CONTENTS

PART 3: MEDITATION ON PERCEPTION

FOREWORD

THE FUNDAMENTAL BUDDHIST teaching of the Four Noble Truths shows that it is craving, the blind thirst for self-centered enjoyment, which underlies all suffering and drives the cycle of repeated birth and death, *saṃsāra*. In other teachings, however, the Buddha points out that the causal relationship between craving and suffering is not final. Craving is itself conditioned, originating from a still deeper root known as ignorance. The Pali word for ignorance, *avijjā*, is a negation meaning the absence of accurate knowledge (*vijjā*). This indicates that what underlies craving and other defiled emotions—such as hatred, anger, pride, and envy—is a failure in cognition. We drift in the current of craving because we do not understand things correctly, because we lack "knowledge and vision of things as they actually are."

Though the word "ignorance" is a negation, in the bustle of our daily lives ignorance takes on an active role, issuing in distorted modes of understanding that turn "upside down" our lived experience of the world. Under the control of ignorance, our cognitive faculties filter the world in such a way that things that are really impermanent, deficient, empty of self, and repulsive appear to us as their exact opposites: as permanent, as enjoyable, as our true self, and as desirable. These "inversions" or distorted modes of cognition operate at several levels. At the coarsest level they determine our fixed views; more deeply, they infest our concepts and thoughts; and most deeply, they govern even our perceptions. Thus we not only conceive things in a distorted manner, but we even perceive the world around us, and most intimately, our own being, as testimony to these flawed notions of permanence, enjoyment, selfhood, and sensual beauty.

We can discern in this process an intricate pattern of causation. Below the threshold of conscious awareness, ignorance infiltrates our perceptions, and from there spreads to our thoughts and views, resulting in distorted modes of understanding. These distorted modes of understanding provoke and reinforce craving along with attachment, aversion, conceit, and other defilements, which then bind us more tightly to the cycle of repeated birth and death. And as we wander on from one life to the next, again and again we encounter the myriad forms of suffering: old age, illness, and death, sorrow, dejection, and despair.

Given this pattern of causation, the path to release from suffering involves not only a sustained volitional effort to resist the lure of craving but a parallel attempt to transform cognition. The ultimate aim in cultivating the Buddha's path is to arrive at a cognitive breakthrough that uproots ignorance from its nest in the deep recesses of the mind. This requires a carefully designed strategy. To achieve final victory it is necessary not only to rupture the causal link between feeling and craving—which is highlighted in many suttas—but to reverse the sequence that leads from ignorance to distorted views. This means that our perceptions must be transformed. Perception must be reoriented so that, instead of seeing things in ways that reinforce craving and other defiled attitudes, we perceive in ways that debilitate craving and ultimately eliminate ignorance.

The path to final freedom can thus be understood in part as a process by which we learn to recognize distorted perceptions for what they are and replace them with correct perceptions. This is a demanding project of mental training, but the Buddha's discourses provide us with guideposts to the kinds of perception we must develop. These perceptions (*saññā*) are at the same time contemplations. In fact, the Pali word usually translated as "contemplation," *anupassanā*, literally means close and repeated (*anu*) seeing (*passanā*). It is this training in close seeing, sustained and repeated over time, that culminates in *vipassanā*, insight or "special seeing." And it is insight that leads to the wisdom of the world-transcending path, which brings the fruit of ultimate liberation.

Among the early collections of the Buddha's discourses, emphasis on the training in right perception appears most prominently in the Aṅguttara Nikāya, the Collection of Numerical Discourses, where the sequence of chapters is governed by an ascending numerical scheme, from the Ones to the Elevens. Several series of texts running through the later chapters of this collection highlight the role of perceptual transformation in facilitating the attainment of nibbāna. The series begins in the Book of Fives, where the Buddha introduces two groups of five perceptions of which he says, "when developed and cultivated, they are of great fruit and benefit, culminating in the deathless, having the deathless as their consummation" (5:61, 5:62). In the Sevens, we again meet two sets of seven perceptions that culminate in the deathless (7:48, 7:49), and so in the Nines (9:16) and the Tens (10:56–57).

In the living Theravāda Buddhist tradition, the best known of the Buddha's discourses on perceptual transformation is the Girimānanda Sutta (Aṅguttara Nikāya 10:60). In this sutta the Buddha teaches ten perceptions, which are really modes of contemplation. He does not merely enumerate them—as he does in the shorter suttas referred to above—but briefly explains what each entails by way of practice. The sutta can thus be seen as a concise compendium of meditation subjects. But the Girimānanda Sutta has achieved popularity for another reason as well: because it was also taught as a "protective discourse" (*paritta*), a source of blessings and a *means* of healing. As the background story to the sutta reveals, the Buddha taught the ten perceptions for the sake of a sick monk named Girimānanda, who is described as "gravely ill," perhaps on the verge of death. And we are told that by the conclusion of the exposition, after Girimānanda learned the ten perceptions, he did in fact recover from his illness.

Buddhist meditation has made its entry into contemporary western culture through the practice of mindfulness, which is often lifted from its original context and presented as a purely secular discipline. It is now taught not only as a vehicle of liberating insight, but for purposes determined by the values of our consumerist society, such as material success, physical health, popularity, and greater efficiency in the workplace. If the Buddha's teachings are to be properly transplanted to their new cultural setting, the basic meditation practices must be made available in their full range and taught in the light of Buddhist philosophical understanding. The Girimānanda Sutta serves this purpose well. The ten perceptions taught in the sutta cover a broad range, extending from the perceptions of impermanence and non-self to the contemplations that lead to dispassion, such as the perceptions of the "impure" nature of the body and the "danger" in our vulnerability to illness and decay. They include reflective meditations on nibbāna and mindfulness of breathing, a tool for developing both tranquility and insight.

The time is ripe for the meditation topics sketched in the Girimānanda Sutta to be explained in detail for those who seek to become better acquainted with the broad expanse of meditation practices taught in the early discourses. With the present book Bhante Gunaratana, a much loved and highly respected meditation teacher, has admirably stepped in to fill this gap. "Bhante G," as he is widely known, possesses the combination of skills needed to fulfill this task. As a monk of Sri Lankan origins, he is deeply grounded in the Pali

Buddhist tradition, especially in the teachings of the Sutta Pitaka, which he imbibed during his years of training at monastic institutions in Sri Lanka. Yet he has lived in the United States for the past forty-five years, and thus is as familiar with American culture as any native-born American from New York, Los Angeles, or the Midwest. His earlier books on meditation have been immensely popular, and for decades he has led meditation retreats for people in this country and around the world.

With these qualifications, he here takes up the task of explaining the Buddhist perspectives on perception, both in its negative role as an instrument of delusion and suffering, and in its positive role as an aid on the path to emancipation. He centers the book on an exposition of the Girimānanda Sutta, which he explains with his characteristic lucidity, in simple and direct language that speaks to the ordinary reader. He repeatedly highlights how these modes of contemplation relate to our everyday experience. Moreover, he explores a theme seldom touched upon by the traditional commentaries on the sutta: how these subjects of meditation can lead to the healing of illness, the Buddha's original purpose in expounding these perceptions for the monk Girimānanda.

Bhante Gunaratana brings to life for the reader of today this ancient discourse of the Buddha, showing us how these teachings, given twenty-five centuries ago, are still just as relevant to us in these times of confusion and uncertainty. Whether or not these perceptions can heal bodily illness is of secondary importance. What is of prime importance is their ability to heal the most debilitating illness of all, the ignorance inherent in mental distortions and in toxic views about ourselves and the world in which we live.

Ven. Bhikkhu Bodhi

PUBLISHER'S ACKNOWLEDGMENT

THE PUBLISHER GRATEFULLY acknowledges the generous contribution of the Hershey Family Foundation toward the publication of this book.

ACKNOWLEDGMENTS

I AM EVER GRATEFUL to Steve Sonnefeld for the generous gift of his time and patience. This book could not have come into being without his extensive hard work on its development. I am thankful to Douglas Imbrogno for his kind assistance in preparation of the manuscript for Wisdom Publications. I am grateful to Brenda Rosen for her painstaking editorial work and to Josh Bartok and Andy Francis for numerous suggestions for polishing and publishing this book. Also I am grateful to Ven. Ethkandawaka Saddajeewa for suggesting that I write a book on this topic. Lastly, I am very grateful to Venerable Bhikkhu Bodhi for taking some of his most precious time to write the foreword to this book.

Bhante Henepola Gunaratana
Forest Meditation Center, Bhavana Society
West Virginia

INTRODUCTION

IN THIS LITTLE BOOK, I focus on how perception can be used as an object of meditation. In Buddhist teachings, perception is one of the basic constituents of the body and mind. It includes the information we get from our five senses and from thought, imagination, and other internal sources, as well as the way the mind processes and understands this information. Like the other constituents of the body and mind described by the Buddha—form, feeling, thought, and consciousness—perception can be trained and ultimately purified through the practice of meditation. When we understand what perception is and how it impacts our lives, we can use it, just as we do any other object of meditation, to overcome harmful ways of thinking and acting and to develop spiritually.

One of the important sources of the Buddha's teachings on perception is the Girimananda Sutta (Anguttara Nikaya, 10:60). As the sutta tells us, once when the Buddha was living at Savatthi, a city of ancient India, the Venerable Girimananda, one of his monks or *bhikkhus*, was afflicted with a painful disease. The Buddha's close disciple, the Venerable Ananda, approached the Buddha and requested that he visit Girimananda out of compassion for his suffering. Instead, the Buddha asked Ananda to go to Girimananda and speak to him about the ten perceptions. "It is possible," the Buddha explained, "that having heard the ten perceptions, the bhikkhu Girimananda would immediately be cured of his illness."

These ten perceptions, which I discuss later in detail, are fundamentally a method of meditation. The tenth perception, mindfulness of in-breathing and out-breathing, is itself a complete meditation practice. As we work through meditation on the ten perceptions, we train the mind to move beyond ordinary, superficial perception into the enlightened perspective that leads to permanent liberation from confusion and unhappiness.

Actually, the instructions in the Girimananda Sutta ask us to engage in two types of meditation. Perhaps we are more familiar with the first of these types, which the Buddha called *samatha* or concentration meditation. Sometimes translated as tranquility meditation or calm abiding, samatha meditation involves gently focusing the mind on one object or experience, such as a candle flame, a prayer or chant, a picture of the Buddha, or simply, as in the Girimananda Sutta, on our regular cycle of breathing in and breathing out. As the mind settles peacefully on this single point of focus, our normal emotional turmoil subsides, and the mind stops its uncontrolled wandering and becomes calm and serene.

The second type of meditation is called *vipassana* or insight meditation. In this technique, mindfulness is used as a tool to increase our awareness of what is happening right now. Over years of vipassana practice, the focused mind gradually penetrates the wall of illusion that separates ordinary awareness from deep understanding of the way we exist. As our insight deepens, we realize that no part of us—not our body, feelings, perceptions, thoughts, or consciousness—is as concrete and permanent as we habitually believe. Like everything else, these parts are always changing and are for that reason sources of discomfort or disease—what the Buddha called "suffering."

The basic process of meditation on perception is quite straightforward. We use tranquility meditation to become calm and centered and insight meditation to understand more clearly how we ordinarily perceive our own body and mind as well as the world around us. To our dismay, we discover that although the way we sense and think about our experiences seems to be solid and reliable, it is, in fact, distorted or mistaken in several important ways. It leads not to clarity and joy but to bewilderment and unhappiness. This understanding motivates us to engage in further meditation with the aim of cultivating purified perception as explained by the Buddha. As a result of these efforts, we progress on the path that leads to freeing ourselves once and for all from illness, confusion, and other forms of physical and mental suffering.

These two types of meditation have been the subject of my teaching and writing for many years. In *Mindfulness in Plain English*, I present a simple, step-by-step guide to mindfulness meditation. Mindfulness, so widely taught and practiced these days as an aid to stress-relief, relaxation, and healing, is actually vipassana or insight meditation, a set of mental activities aimed at experiencing uninterrupted awareness of what is happening moment to moment. *Eight Mindful Steps to Happiness* encourages readers to use mindfulness meditation to progress along the Buddha's eight-step path from suffering to permanent happiness. In *Beyond Mindfulness in Plain English*, I explain how concentration meditation can help us transcend ordinary consciousness and reach highly purified and luminous mental states on the path. My most recent book, *The Four Foundations of Mindfulness*, discusses the Satipatthana Sutta, the Buddha's clearest and most succinct presentation of mindfulness meditation.

Though each of these books presents basic meditation instructions, the subject is so important that I conclude this introduction with a simple way to practice samatha or concentration meditation drawn from the Girimananda Sutta, so that readers can try meditation themselves. Those who need more detailed guidance or help dealing with physical pain, distractions, and other problems might find *Mindfulness in Plain*

English to be a good resource. As I mentioned, the Girimananda Sutta also presents a method of vipassana or insight meditation. In essence, the sutta reveals how a combination of concentration meditation and insight meditation can help us achieve vibrant mental health as well as physical and emotional healing. To that end, this book includes several sets of step-by-step instructions for engaging in mindfulness meditation on the perception of impermanence.

Readers can expect a range of positive results from engaging in meditation on perception. On the everyday level, cultivating mindfulness can help us overcome disturbing mental attitudes, such as anger, greed, and jealousy, and increase positive and healthy feelings, such as patience, loving-friendliness, and peace of mind. We become more impartial and objective observers of what is taking place within our minds and in the world around us and, for this reason, can more easily sidestep situations that might lead to anxiety and unhappiness.

On the spiritual level, meditation on perception can help us make steady progress on the path toward liberation from suffering. It can also result in genuine healing. We could say that the Girimananda Sutta is not a faith-healing system but a truth-healing system. Perhaps it works something like this: When we listen to the truth, we become glad. When we appreciate the truth we hear, our insight is deepened, and the mind prompts the brain and body to generate healing chemicals. Though meditation should never be regarded as a substitute for medical treatment, many people have found it to be a valuable therapeutic complement to traditional care.

Looking ahead, we begin by exploring how perception works and where this faculty fits in the Buddha's description of reality. Then we turn to the Girimananda Sutta and examine in detail the ten perceptions the Buddha asked Ananda to relate to Girimananda. For each of the ten, I begin with a quotation from the sutta so that readers can experience the Buddha's words firsthand. Finally, we consider how we can use the method of insight meditation on perception the Buddha prescribed for Girimananda for personal and spiritual healing. But first we turn to the sutta itself for practical advice about meditation.

Getting Started with Meditation

The initial meditation instructions in the Girimananda Sutta are deceptively simple. As the Buddha explained to Ananda, in mindfulness of breathing, the meditator does the following:

> Here, a bhikkhu, having gone to the forest, to the foot of a tree, or to an empty hut, sits down. Having folded his legs crosswise, straightened his body, and established mindfulness in front of him, just mindful he breathes in, mindful he breathes out.
>
> Breathing in long, he knows: 'I breathe in long'; or breathing out long, he knows: 'I breathe out long.' Breathing in short, he knows: 'I breathe in short'; or breathing out short, he knows: 'I breathe out short.' (tr. Bhikkhu Bodhi)

So how should we get started with meditation based on these instructions?

▸ **Go to a quiet place.** Though the Buddha suggested a forest, the foot of a tree, or an empty abode, for us, the place simply needs to be somewhere we can be alone, away from everyday concerns. It will not help us to develop concentration if we take our mobile phone or laptop along! In order to focus our attention, we need to avoid distractions, both inner and outer.

▸ **Adopt a stable and comfortable posture.** The Buddha recommended sitting down, folding the legs, and straightening the back. Many people today practice meditation while sitting cross-legged on the floor, supported by a low cushion. But it is also possible to meditate while sitting upright in a chair, or even, when circumstances make it preferable, while standing up, walking, or lying down. The goal is for the body to be settled and relaxed, and for the posture to be one we can easily sustain for an extended period of time without shifting or readjusting.

▸ **Bring attention to the present moment.** As the Buddha expressed this guideline, we should set up mindfulness "in front." We follow this instruction by remembering that the past is gone and the future has not yet arrived. The only time we can be truly present is right in front of us, the moment that is happening now.

▸ **Focus the mind on the breath, coming in and going out.** A single point of focus helps the mind to settle down. The best place to experience the movement of the breath is the spot where the flow of air touches or rubs the rim of the nostrils during inhalation and exhalation.

▸ **Become aware that sometimes the breath is long, and other times it is short.** This instruction does not mean that we should try to control our breathing, forcing ourselves to take long inhalations and exhalations or short ones. Rather, we should pay attention to natural variations in the rhythm of our breathing. Buddhist meditation is not a breathing exercise. Rather, we are using the breath, something that is always with us, as a point of focus for the mind to help us develop concentration and mindfulness.

▸ **Be gentle and consistent.** Meditation is often called "practice." This word reminds us that we cannot expect to be expert meditators the first time we try it, or even the second, third, or tenth time. Choose a time when it is possible to be quiet and free of distractions. Many people find that early morning, before they get engaged in the concerns of the day, or evening, if that is a time when they feel awake and alert, are good choices. Establishing a regular time and place to meditate each day is a gentle way to encourage and support our practice.

▶ **Be flexible and positive.** Make sure that the meditation period is long enough to give the mind time to settle down. Many people find that meditating for twenty or thirty minutes each day works well, but even five or ten minutes is OK on days when we are especially busy. The longer we sit and focus on the breath, the more relaxed and comfortable we should feel. It will not help us to regard meditation as a chore or obligation. Rather it should be an activity we look forward to and enjoy because of the relaxation and pleasure it brings to the body and mind and how much it helps us personally and spiritually.

PART 1: PERCEPTION

· 1 ·

WHAT IS PERCEPTION?

FOR THE BUDDHA, perception is pure and simple. When the eyes
see a visual object, they do so without embellishment. As the Buddha explained to his monks in the *Connected Discourses*:

> And why, bhikkhus, do you call it perception? It perceives,
> bhikkhus; therefore, it is called perception. And what does
> it perceive? It perceives blue, it perceives yellow, it perceives
> red, it perceives white. It perceives, bhikkhus; therefore, it
> is called perception. (tr. Bhikkhu Bodhi)

The type of perception that conveys information such as the color of an
object is called eye-perception. As the Buddha explained it, the process
of eye-perception works like this: When an eye that is open meets any
form or visual object, such as a flower, consciousness arises in the mind.
The meeting of the three—the eye, the flower, and consciousness—is
called contact. Depending on contact, feeling arises. Feeling is one of
the five factors that make up mentality: contact, feeling, perception,
thought, and attention. What we feel, we perceive. Then we think of
what is perceived. Thinking begins the process of judgment that leads
to mental proliferation.

Imagine, for instance, that there is a flower in front of our eyes.
Our eyes encounter the flower as soon as they are opened. Visual consciousness immediately arises. In dependence on these three—the eye,

the flower, and visual consciousness—visual contact occurs. Pleasant, unpleasant, or neutral feeling arises depending on this visual contact. Now the mind has perceived or cognized the flower. Thoughts such as "I like this color," or "I don't like this color," appear in the mind depending on its color, such as blue, yellow, red, or white. Depending on the colors of flowers that we have seen in the past, or colors of flowers that we would see in future, our minds begin to proliferate more and more thoughts. The proliferation of thought can move in many different directions according to the flower's shape, size, significance, chemical composition, usages, where it grows, how it grows, and so on. In the same way, mental proliferation goes on with sounds, smells, tastes, touches, and thoughts. So visual perception is actually the combination of the eye, form, consciousness, contact, attention, and feeling.

Consciousness, of course, refers to the mind and its activities. It is the base for other mental factors to function. Contact arises only when the senses, sensory objects, and consciousness are present. Attention is a mental factor that purposefully engages consciousness to focus on a particular object. Feeling is followed by perception. Then we think about what is perceived. Thinking is any intentional mind state and includes both thoughts and emotional responses. If consciousness is not present, feeling, perceiving, thinking, and paying attention to anything do not arise.

The same mental processes occur with regard to all of our senses. In Buddhist thought, there are six sense organs: the eyes, ears, nose, tongue, body, and mind. So, for instance, the combination of the ear, sound, consciousness, contact, and feeling arouses perception of sound. Similarly, the meeting of the nose and smell, the tongue and taste, the body and touch, and the mind and mental objects, such as ideas, thoughts, mental pictures, or emotions, arouses consciousness, contact, feeling, attention, and thus, perception.

The function of perception is cognizing or, to use a more familiar word, recognizing an object. Because the process of cognition happens so quickly, we may not realize that each act of perception involves a series of internal mental steps that help us to understand something. Perception actually takes place in the mind. On the simplest level, meditation on perception gives us the opportunity to become aware of the role the mind and its activities play in determining our perceptions, and more important, in determining what we say and do in response to our perceptions.

Perception is so influential because in addition to determining the apparent characteristics of objects or mental pictures of objects, such as their color, shape, size, or hardness, the thought that follows perception also judges whether the things we perceive are pleasant, unpleasant, or neither. The Buddha taught that desire or craving arise naturally in an untrained mind when it encounters what it takes to be pleasant, beautiful, or attractive. Dislike or aversion arise when the mind encounters what it takes to be unpleasant, ugly, or repulsive. We generally ignore or pay little attention to what we perceive to be neither pleasant nor unpleasant. As we discover, sensory objects in themselves are not marked with beauty or ugliness, pleasantness or unpleasantness, attractiveness or unattractiveness. It is the thinking about what is perceived that judges or categorizes them and thus guides our responses.

When we examine the perception process with careful mindfulness, we become aware that perception operates on the basis of previous information that has been stored in the mind. Memories and past experiences prompt the mind to generate reasons that explain why we believe that something we perceive is beautiful or ugly. Today there is a whole system of education—art and music appreciation classes, for instance, and even cooking shows on television—that teaches us to categorize and judge various sights, sounds, smells, tastes, touches, and ideas. However, any judgments we form about the things we perceive are our own mental constructs. Though we believe that the characteristics we ascribe to objects and experiences are part of the objects themselves—large or small, delicious or distasteful, harmonious or discordant—closer examination reveals that these attributions are artificial and personal. Mindful attention that aims to purify perception is attention without such personal additions, and without craving, aversion, and other delusions.

We can prove to ourselves that perception is artificial and personal by remembering how often people disagree about the beauty or ugliness, deliciousness or distastefulness, pleasantness or unpleasantness, of a particular work of art, architectural style, item of clothing, type of food, or musical composition. Moreover, opinions often vary over time and space, from decade to decade, from country to country, and from earlier points in our life to later ones. For instance, we might have disliked classical music when we were younger, but now it is our favorite. Our perceptions also change according to circumstances. Yellow roses might look very beautiful when we see them in a summer garden, but seem unpleasant and even cause us pain when we see them at the funeral of a friend. In the same way, when we are ill, foods that we enjoyed on many occasions might seem disgusting or repulsive.

So, we might be wondering, what is true and reliable about our perceptions? According to the Buddha, the only natural characteristics of any object or experience are that it is impermanent, unsatisfactory, and selfless. Impermanence points to the truth that over time, everything changes, breaks down, or dies. No person is exempt; no one lives forever, not even the Buddha. No thing is exempt; no matter how solid and enduring our senses perceive a mountain to be, every second it is wearing down. Because everything alters or disappears, nothing that exists can give us lasting satisfaction. The more attached we are to something or someone, the more unhappy we are when it is gone. We lose a favorite piece of jewelry. A family member passes away. Because everything is impermanent, everything is unsatisfactory.

For the same reason, because everything is always changing, the Buddha also said that things are selfless. As we noted, nothing that we perceive is beautiful or ugly, desirable or detestable, as a natural characteristic. Things and people, including you and me, are always in process, always in flux. What rises in our estimation eventually falls; whatever we love eventually we lose; what makes us happy eventually causes us suffering. Precisely because their identity is not fixed and their qualities are not solid and enduring, we say that everything that exists lacks self or soul.

The conclusion that follows from this understanding points to the path we must follow if we wish to free ourselves from suffering. Training in mindfulness meditation and using the insights it provides to perceive the impermanence of people and objects protects us from experiencing the desire to hang on to them. Gradually, we come to see that suffering is a mental state. It arises in us, not in the objects we perceive. For this reason, the Buddha has said, desire and craving—specifically desire and craving for impermanent, unsatisfactory, and selfless things—is the cause of suffering. Meditation on perception helps us to reach this profound realization.

Perception and the Aggregates

As we mentioned, perception is one of the five basic constituents of the body and mind described by the Buddha—form, feeling, perception, thought, and consciousness. These constituents, generally called the "five aggregates," include every possible aspect of reality. Form refers to every material thing that our senses can perceive, including the various parts of our own body.

The four other aggregates include all experiences of the mind. Feeling, as we have seen, can be pleasant, unpleasant, or neutral. Thoughts, memories, imaginative wandering, and dreams can arise depending on which of these feelings we feel. When we have a delicious dinner we remember it and may think about it. When we have unpleasant feelings, our thoughts and memories about them also tend to be unpleasant. As we said, feeling arises in the mind because of contact between the senses, an object or mental picture, and consciousness. As we have also said, the aggregate of perception arises in the mind as a result of the combination of the senses, an exterior or interior object, contact, consciousness, attention, and feeling.

The aggregate thought includes every kind of mental activity, including ideas, fantasies, fears, and emotional responses. It is easiest to understand this aggregate if we consider that thoughts are simply "mental objects" that we perceive internally. It's also important to recognize that some thoughts are positive and helpful, such as loving-friendliness and faith in the Buddha and his teachings, and others are unwholesome and hurtful, such as anger and skeptical doubt that the Buddha's teachings can make a difference in our lives.

The fifth aggregate, consciousness, is perhaps the most difficult to comprehend. Consciousness is basic awareness or knowing. Sometimes we use the word "mind" to describe this function. According to the Buddha, consciousness or mind is luminous, which means that it shines light on things, including our perceptions. In fact, there is no such thing as mere mind or mere consciousness. We infer the existence of mind or consciousness based solely on its contents. Thus we can say that consciousness is always associated with a perception, thought, emotion, or some other mental object.

Meditation on Perception and the Aggregates

One of the best ways to experience the five aggregates is to be mindful of them while practicing meditation on the breath as explained in the introduction. Mindfulness meditation on perception of the five aggregates is based on the Buddha's instructions to his bhikkhus. As the Buddha instructed in the Dhammapada, his teachings—the true *Dhamma*—should be perceived in one's own body:

> One does not uphold the Dhamma
> Only because one speaks a lot.
> Having heard even a little,
> If one perceives the Dhamma with one's own body,
> And is never negligent of the Dhamma,
> Then one is indeed an upholder of the Dhamma.
> (tr. Gil Fronsdal)

Here is how we might practice this type of meditation:

- ► As we focus on our regular cycle of inhalation and exhalation, we gently direct our attention to perceiving each of the five aggregates.
- ► We become mindful that the breath itself is the aggregate of form. Our senses perceive the flow of air entering and leaving the body, both at the rim of the nostrils and as the abdomen rises and falls with each inhalation and exhalation. We also may experience the

body as form because of pain in our back or knee as we sit.

- ► We become mindful of the aggregate of feeling by perceiving the slight discomfort or anxiety we experience when our lungs are empty and the slight pleasure we feel when we inhale again.

- ► We become mindful of the aggregate of perception by perceiving the physical sensations of the breath and the pleasant and unpleasant feelings arising from the breath.

- ► We become mindful of the aggregate of thought by noticing any thoughts, such as faith or doubt, and emotions, such as loving-friendliness or impatience, that arise while we are breathing.

- ► We become mindful of the aggregate of consciousness by perceiving alterations in the other four aggregates as we breathe—changing sensations in the body, feelings of pleasure and discomfort, perception of external and internal objects, and the arising and passing away of thoughts and emotions. We see that consciousness itself is changing moment to moment. In fact, all five aggregates are always changing in gross and subtle ways.

- ► Our goal is to perceive whatever arises and passes away with an impartial attitude, neither clinging to experiences of pleasure nor pushing away experiences of discomfort. This neutral attitude is the key to mindfulness. As we discover, it is impossible for us to focus the mind on any meditation object unless we perceive it impartially. When we allow feelings of pleasure and discomfort to color our perceptions, the perceptions themselves rise to the forefront of consciousness, and our awareness of the breath goes on the backburner.

- ► The most important aspect of this meditation is becoming mindful of each fleeting moment of perception marked by impermanence. As our meditation practice deepens, we gain experience in maintaining focus on the breath, perceiving physical sensations, feelings, thoughts, and emotions as impermanent, while at the same time remaining mindful of impartial perceptions.

Why Impartial Perception Is Important

Cultivating impartial perception during meditation is so important because the desire that arises in the mind for any of the five aggregates blocks our ability to liberate ourselves from suffering. As one of the Buddha's monks, the Venerable Mahakaccana, explained to Haliddakani, a householder or layperson, perception is a "home of consciousness," as are the other aggregates. Craving and other colorations are like chains that bind us to the aggregates, and thus to life after life characterized by impermanence and dissatisfaction. As the Buddha said in the Haliddakani Sutta:

> The form element, householder, is the home of consciousness; one whose consciousness is shackled by lust for the form element is called one who roams about in a home. The feeling element is the home of consciousness . . . The perception element is the home of consciousness . . . The volitional formations [thought] element is the home of consciousness; one whose consciousness is shackled by lust for the volitional formations element is called one who roams about in a home. It is in such a way that one roams about in a home. (tr. Bhikkhu Bodhi)

As our mindfulness becomes more stable, we discover that the entire Dhamma is inscribed in our body and mind. If we focus our minds only on the perception of external things, we don't see the Dhamma that we carry around with us all our lives. We are like a blind person walking around with a bag full of diamonds, unaware of how valuable this heavy bag is. When we focus instead on perception of our own body and mind, we discover that we carry a treasure. Discovering these inner riches, we find nothing less than the path to liberation, permanent freedom from suffering.

· 2 ·

DISTORTED PERCEPTION

AS WE HAVE SAID, in its own nature, perception is pure and clean. Yet it is also quite delicate and vulnerable to being distorted by the virus of concepts. Every day, our minds are bombarded with countless concepts. Ideas, memories, and imaginings from past experiences, sensory information from current experiences, and fantasies and daydreams about future plans are always arising and passing away. Every day we spend many hours talking, reading, learning, and listening to others. All of this information creates a vast number of concepts in our minds. The Buddha explained that holding too many concepts—what we could call "conceptual proliferation"—confuses our perceptions. As we said, perception arises after feeling. As soon as we perceive an external or internal object, feelings arise based on concepts stored in the mind, coloring our perception and obstructing our ability to see clearly what something is.

Let's consider an example. Suppose we see someone's nose. Concepts stored previously in the mind arise to our consciousness and make us believe that the nose is beautiful or ugly. Next we see the person's lips. Again, our previously stored information makes us believe that the lips are beautiful or ugly. Similarly, we see the person's eyes, eyebrows, teeth, head hair, body hair, and skin. Our mind has stored many concepts concerning each of these visual objects. All this information fuels our positive or negative judgment of the person's features. When we add all of these conceptual judgments together, we believe that we are seeing a beautiful face or an ugly face. Similarly, we add numerous concepts with regard to hands, legs, fingers, nails, and every other part of the person's body. As a result, we decide that we have seen a beautiful or an ugly person.

But in reality, all that we have perceived are eyes, nose, teeth, skin, hair, hands, legs, and face in the conventional sense. These body parts are in themselves neither beautiful nor ugly; nor is the person as a whole beautiful or ugly. What has happened is that concepts, ideas, opinions, beliefs, and many other categories of conditioning have influenced our perception. In essence, our perception has become distorted. Only if we can transcend these distortions can we perceive the simple truth of what appears to the senses.

Distorted perception is a problem because it leads to attachment and aversion. We become attached to or crave whatever we mistakenly believe will bring lasting happiness to ourselves. We push away or hate whatever we mistakenly believe will harm us or make our lives unhappy. These judgments are faulty because nothing impermanent can bring us lasting happiness or lasting unhappiness. Moreover, like other attributes supplied by the mind during the process of perception, "myself," "me," and "my" are concepts that are essentially artificial and personal. Though we believe them to be part of whatever it is that we perceive, they are actually distortions supplied by the mind.

Suppose, for example, we see a photograph. What we have actually perceived, as the Buddha defined perception, is a piece of paper with color and imagery on one side, or an image made up of colored dots of light on a computer screen. But what we see instead is "my photo," "me," or "the image of myself." Nowhere in the photograph or computer image are the concepts "me," "mine," or "myself." These ideas come from conceptual information previously stored in the mind. We add these concepts to the photograph, conditioning our pure perception so that we develop attachment or aversion for various parts of "my" image, such as "my beautiful shiny hair" or "my ugly double chin." Mindfulness meditation helps us to see that concepts arise from the mind and not from the object being perceived. Everything is subject to change. Something that we regard as "me" or "mine" is just an impermanent object of perception, nothing more.

The implications of this realization are far-reaching. How many problems spring from the concepts "my" country and "my" religion? How do we react when something threatens one of the objects or people in our lives that we regard as "mine"? Every kind of conflict from family fights to world wars has its origins in distorted concepts. Family members argue over a piece of artwork that each believes belongs to "me." A battle breaks out over a piece of land two countries regard as "mine."

Like a Mirage

Distorted perceptions are like a mirage. Deceived by a mirage, a deer runs quickly toward what it perceives as water. As he runs, he sees that the water-like mirage is still far ahead of him. So he keeps running toward it to drink. When he is even more tired and thirsty, he stops and looks back. Then he sees that he has gone past the water. When he runs back, he perceives that the water is ahead of him. So he runs back and forth until he is exhausted and falls to the ground.

Distorted perception is like that for us. Pulled by our own attachments, we are always chasing phantoms. Terrified, we run away from monsters created from our own aversions. So long as perception is distorted, we are unable to see the true nature of what is in front of us—nothing but an ever-changing collection of sights, sounds, smells, tastes, touches, and thoughts or concepts. Moreover, nothing that we perceive has a self or soul; and nothing can bring us permanent happiness or unhappiness.

In essence, when perception is distorted, we perceive impermanence as permanence, suffering as happiness, something neither beautiful nor ugly as beautiful or ugly, or something not self as self. The suffering we cause ourselves by this distortion is illustrated by a story in the suttas. Once, an eighty-year-old devotee of the Buddha known as Nakulapita was experiencing a lot of pain. He went to see the Buddha to get some advice. Nakulapita said:

> "I am old, venerable sir, aged, burdened with years, advanced in life, come to the last stage, afflicted in body, often ill. I rarely get to see the Blessed One and the bhikkhus worthy of esteem. Let the Blessed One exhort me, venerable sir, let him instruct me, since that would lead to my welfare and happiness for a long time."
>
> "So it is, householder, so it is!" the Buddha replied. "This body of yours is afflicted, weighed down, encumbered. If anyone carrying around this body were to claim to be healthy even for a moment, what is that due to other than foolishness? Therefore, householder, you should train yourself thus: 'Even though I am afflicted in body, my mind will be unafflicted.' Thus should you train yourself." (Nakulapita Sutta, tr. Bhikkhu Bodhi)

Nakulapita did not comprehend the complete meaning of this brief teaching, but he did not ask the Buddha any further questions out of respect. He got up and went to see the Venerable Sariputta, one of the

Buddha's close disciples, and asked him to explain the meaning of the Buddha's brief statement.

Venerable Sariputta said, "A person who is unfamiliar with the teaching of the Buddha regards the five aggregates as his self. With the change and decay of these aggregates, there arises in him sorrow, lamentation, pain, grief, and despair. Thus he is afflicted both in body and in mind."

Elucidating this truth with regards to each of the five aggregates, Sariputta explained the suffering caused by distorted perception: A man "regards perception as self, or self as possessing perception, or perception as in self, or self as in perception. He lives obsessed by the notions: 'I am perception, perception is mine.' As he lives obsessed by these notions, that perception of his changes and alters. With the change and alteration of perception, there arise in him sorrow, lamentation, pain, grief, and despair."

But, Sariputta concluded, "A noble disciple who has heard the Dhamma does not regard the aggregates as his self. The aggregates may change, but sorrow, lamentation, pain, grief, and despair do not arise in him. Thus, though he may be afflicted in body, he is not afflicted in mind."

Nakulapita's lesson applies to us as well. We lament when we perceive the signs of aging like gray hair and wrinkles, forgetting that this impermanent body has been aging every day since we were born. People and possessions we believe to be inherently beautiful, permanently pleasurable, and capable of bringing us lasting happiness are also always changing. Beauty fades, and what used to bring us pleasure now causes us difficulty and pain. As Nakulapita discovered and we must as well, perception is not the self. Our internal perceptions of our body, feelings, thoughts, and mind as well as our external perceptions of the world around us are always changing, as are the things we perceive.

Nothing is "me" or "mine." If it were, we would be able to control what we perceive and avoid those perceptions that cause us suffering. As the Buddha said in the Anattalakkhana Sutta:

> Bhikkhus, perception is not-self. If perception were self, then perception would not be prone to affliction, and it would be possible to say, "Let my perception be thus; let my perception not be thus." Because perception is not-self, perception is prone to affliction, and it is not possible to say, "Let my perception be thus; let my perception not be thus." (tr. Bhikkhu Bodhi)

The same is true for each of the other aggregates. The body is not the self; feelings are not the self; thoughts are not the self; consciousness is not the self. Like our perceptions, all of the aggregates are changing all the time.

Perceptual Knots

Distorted perceptions are called "knots" because they keep us tied to life after life filled with impermanence and suffering. The Buddha identified four kinds of perceptual knots. The first, perception of clinging to the pleasant, is attachment to things that we mistakenly believe will bring us lasting happiness or pleasure. For instance, no bride and groom expect to become bitter enemies fighting over their possessions within a few years! The opposite, perception of pushing away the unpleasant, is aversion for things we mistakenly believe will always be distressing or painful. For example, we don't expect the neighbor with whom we have had angry arguments to be the person who saves our life when the house catches fire.

The third perceptual knot is perception of cruelty. This knot calls attention to harmful actions based on distorted perceptions. When our perception of pushing away the unpleasant develops into anger and hatred, we sometimes act out cruelly by engaging in harsh speech or even in physical violence. We see this knot operating in fights between people and nations. The fourth knot is called "wrong view." Wrong view, or ignorance as it is sometimes called, refers to our mistaken perception that people and objects are permanent, that they can give us lasting happiness or misery, and that they possess a self or soul. We can say that wrong view lies at the root of every kind of deluded perception.

It is easy to see why these perceptual knots obstruct our ability to liberate ourselves from life after life of impermanence and suffering. Because of these knots, we engage in harmful actions of body, speech, and mind. These actions create *kamma* (or karma), which is simply the natural law of cause and effect. If the cause is negative, the effect is bound to be negative as well. In other words, our own negative kamma is the cause of our remaining in a condition of suffering. The mind of a person who has attained liberation   freedom from all dissatisfaction—is free from perceptual knots or ties. As the Buddha said in the Magandhiya Sutta:

> There are no knots for those who have abandoned perceptions. There are no delusions for those who are liberated from all knots. Those who hold on to perceptions and delusion move in the world with conflicts.

The perceptions the Buddha urged us to abandon are not the simple and pure perceptions he described as perceiving blue, perceiving yellow, perceiving red, perceiving white. Rather we are urged to abandon the perceptions colored by feeling that lead us to cling to the pleasant and push away the unpleasant. We react this way because the fourth perceptual knot, wrong view, causes us to perceive that things are permanent, inherently pleasant or unpleasant, and possess a self or soul. These delusions, as the Buddha said, cause us to "move in the world with conflicts."

The Buddha explained this problem in more detail in the sutta known as "The Honeyball" (Madhupindika Sutta). At that time, the Buddha was living near Kapilavatthu in the Banyan Park. One evening, one of his bhikkhus asked him, "Lord, what sort of doctrine is it where one does not keep quarreling with anyone in the world ... where perceptions no longer obsess?" The Buddha answered as follows:

> Bhikkhu, as to the source through which perceptions and notions born of mental proliferation beset a man: if nothing is found there to delight in, welcome and hold to, this is the end of the underlying tendency to lust, of the underlying tendency to aversion, of the underlying tendency to views, of the underlying tendency to doubt, of the underlying tendency to conceit, of the underlying tendency to desire for being, of the underlying tendency to ignorance; this is the end of resorting to rods and weapons, of quarrels, brawls, disputes, recrimination, malicious words, and false speech; here these evil unwholesome states cease without remainder. (tr. Bhikkhu Bodhi)

In other words, interpretations of perceptions lead to all sorts of conflicts. Kings argue with kings, politicians with politicians, parents with children, children with parents, siblings with siblings, uncles and aunts with nephews and nieces, neighbors with neighbors, and countries with countries.

The Buddha's solution to this problem is straightforward: We train ourselves to use mindfulness to focus on the simple cognitive aspects of perception without going beyond them into judgments and interpretations. We remind ourselves that conceptual proliferation gets in the way of clear perception and always strive to perceive things impartially. We remain mindful that our perceptions, like every other part of the mind and body, are always changing and will never bring us permanent satisfaction or dissatisfaction. When we understand deeply that the intrinsic nature of all perceptions is impermanent, unsatisfactory, and selfless, there is no room for conflict!

· 3 ·

PURIFIED PERCEPTION

IN ORDER to prevent perception from becoming an affliction, the Buddha showed us a way to train it. Mind or consciousness, as we have said, is clean and luminous in itself. But the train of mental activities set in motion when the senses meet sensory objects can make the mind or consciousness unclean. As we have seen, preconceived notions about the objects we perceive color our perceptions with judgments and lead the untrained mind to mental defilements such as craving and hatred. If we wish to overcome these defilements, we must cleanse our perceptions through meditation.

According to the Buddha, perceptions arise and cease in two ways. Some perceptions arise and cease owing to causes and conditions. Due to impermanence, some perceptions come into being and others pass away as the causes and conditions that support their existence change or end. For example, our perception of a gloomy day arises due to a combination of air temperature, wind speed, barometric pressure, precipitation, cloud cover, and other meteorological conditions. When these causes and conditions change and the sun comes out, this perception passes away.

However, other perceptions arise and cease as a result of effort. As the Buddha said, "Some perceptions arise through training, and some pass away through training." A simple example of this process is the way that listening to the Dhamma—which is itself an act of perception—arouses the perception of faith and helps distorted perceptions to pass away. Perhaps we have had the experience of listening very attentively to the reading or chanting of a sutta or to an explanation of its meaning. Our attention is focused so strongly that we understand deeply the meaning of each word we hear. As a result, we develop faith in the Buddha and his teachings. Other miraculous effects including the healing of illness may arise from the perception of hearing the Dhamma. Yet there is no magic in the chanting or recital. Traditional Buddhist discourses are composed of truth, and truth itself has power.

Wishing for the well-being of a person based on the recitation of truth is a well-known practice in Buddhist stories. For instance, when the Venerable Mahakassapa was ill, the Buddha visited him and recited the seven factors of enlightenment (*bojjhanga*). When he heard these words, Mahakassapa was cured. Another sutta tells us that when the Buddha himself was ill, the Venerable Mahacunda recited these same seven factors, and the Buddha's sickness vanished. The seven factors, which are explained later in detail, are mindfulness, investigation into phenomena, energy, joy, tranquility, concentration, and equanimity. These factors arise one after the other as we progress through the high mental states of the meditative path.

Other suttas are traditionally recited on special occasions to invoke peace, happiness, and comfort on behalf of people who are suffering from illness or from emotions such as fear. This practice also is based on traditional stories. The Ratana Sutta says that when the people of the town of Vesali were suffering from disease and famine, they called on the Buddha for help. The Buddha directed his disciple the Venerable Ananda to go through the town reciting a short discourse that proclaimed the truth of the Three Jewels: the enlightened teacher or Buddha, his enlightened teachings or Dhamma, and his community of followers or Sangha. Hearing this recitation led to the end of the town's troubles.

In the next part of this book, we look at another important example of a healing sutta, the recitation of the ten perceptions of the Girimananda Sutta. When the Venerable Girimananda heard these words and contemplated deeply on their meaning, he regained his health.

Mindfulness Cleanses Perception

When we think about using mindfulness to cleanse perception, we might begin by wondering how perception becomes tainted in the first place. In some suttas, the Buddha taught that the taints of craving and hatred that defile the luminous mind come from outside. This teaching implies that the defilements are not in the mind at birth. But according to the Dhamma taught by the Buddha elsewhere, external taints could not invade the mind if the mind did not have the "trace of taints" within it already. What happens is that the mind that has taints in it looks for matching taints outside and gets what it desires.

Where, we might be wondering, do these traces of taints come from? The Buddha taught that this present life of ours is the direct result of kamma, cause and effect. Unwholesome actions that we intentionally committed in past lifetimes are the cause; this present life of impermanence and suffering is the effect. If the mind of our previous life had been free of all taints and traces of taints, we would not have taken rebirth at all. Instead, we would enjoy the state of purity and peace beyond the cycle of suffering rebirths that is called liberation or *nibbana*.

Nibbana is not a location or condition somewhere outside of us. Rather, it is within. Nibbana is the total destruction of all defilements. The very moment our greed, hatred, and ignorance are destroyed, nibbana arises. The key to overcoming defilements and reaching nibbana is cultivating (or training) the mind. As the Buddha said, "As rain does not get into a well thatched house, so craving does not get into a well trained mind."

So how should we proceed? First, we must understand what we are trying to accomplish and develop some skill in mindfulness both during meditation and in life. We use this mindfulness to prevent external defilements from entering the mind by carefully guarding the senses. We also use it to prevent latent tendencies that exist as traces within the mind, such as craving, hatred, greed, jealousy, and pride, from arising. If, in spite of these efforts, latent tendencies do arise or reach the stage of manifestation in words or deeds, we apply additional mindful effort to overcome them.

Then, instead of worrying over past unwholesome thoughts, we arouse wholesome thoughts, such as generosity, patience, and loving-friendliness and use effort to strengthen the wholesome thoughts. In addition, we use mindfulness to guard the senses against external sensory experiences that might stimulate any unwholesome tendencies. As we have said, mindfulness is in essence vipassana or insight meditation. Only insight meditation can train the mind to watch and discipline itself in order to purify it, eventually destroying all the defilements, including their latent tendencies.

Let's consider a practical example of this process:

- Let's say that we are troubled by the perception of hatred that is manifesting as violent anger toward another person who has hurt us in some way. Because of the Dhamma teachings that we have heard and deeply contemplated, we perceive the dangers of engaging in hatred.

- As a result, we observe moral principles that guard the senses. For instance, we use mindfulness to avoid obsessively dwelling on the person with whom we are angry or the circumstances that caused the anger to arise. We also avoid seeing and speaking with the person so that the perception of additional sensory experiences does not stimulate our unwholesome tendency.

▶ Finally, secluded from sensory stimulation, we take up a wholesome meditation subject such as patience or loving-friendliness and dedicate many hours to meditation. Through this activity, we abandon our previous perception of hatred and cultivate a new perception of wholesome factors leading to liberation.

We can apply a similar method to the perception of sensual pleasure that leads to lust and craving, as well as to the perception of restlessness and worry that distract us from our meditation, of sleepiness and drowsiness when we are trying to concentrate, and of skeptical doubt in the Buddha and his teachings. It is important to recognize in this context that while we cannot purify the mind of old defilements, we can try to prevent new defilements from entering the mind. Moreover, meditation can make old defilements weak by not reinforcing them. When they don't get nourishment, the old defilements become weak, ineffective, or even atrophy.

Thus, though we cannot do anything about yesterday's lack of mindfulness, we can remember that we were unmindful yesterday and try to be mindful today. Yesterday's lack of mindfulness allowed greed, hatred, and delusion to enter the mind. These defilements made us unhappy, and we do not wish to allow them to continue. Though we cannot remove them all at once, we can apply mindfulness to chip away at them little by little.

Engaging in this process is, in fact, following the Buddha's path. We are engaging in effort that aims to purify the mind of taints and their traces. As the mind is purified, perception is also purified. As we have seen, perception is one of the five interlinked factors of mental functioning: contact, feeling, attention, thought, and consciousness. Because of the inseparable connection among these five components, any mental state that affects consciousness affects the other functions. It follows that when we perceive something with a purified, luminous mind, our perception also becomes purified and luminous.

Through engaging in mindful attention both during meditation sessions and as we go about our everyday activities, we begin to see how the Buddha's path unfolds. Where is the path, and what is the path? It is within us—within, we might say, the mind and its activities. We will never find the path anywhere else—not in books, not in a shop, not in temples. It is within us. Mindfulness is the key that opens the gate to this road.

Purified Perception and the Path

The first step in walking the Buddha's path is using our perception to hear the Dhamma. The Buddha taught that people are divided into three groups: uninstructed worldly people, instructed worldly people, and instructed noble disciples. Uninstructed worldly people are those who "have not heard." Of course, they have heard many things. Their ears have been exposed to many sounds, and their minds have been filled with many concepts and ideas. But until they hear the right teachings or Dhamma, they are uninstructed persons. This great mass of people will go through repeated births and deaths within the cycle of suffering life after suffering life propelled by kamma. Very few uninstructed worldly people will achieve liberation from this cycle.

Instructed worldly people are those who have used their hearing faculty to listen mindfully to the right message. Yet unless they take action to put to use what they have heard, they have not yet entered the Buddha's path. Instructed noble disciples have not only heard the right teaching, have also examined the meaning of what they have heard and realized its truth. Though they know that the mind is luminous, they understand that the mind still needs to be trained to reach purity. For this reason they practice cultivating the luminous mind to reach purity using the method outlined above. Because practicing this path makes its followers noble, it is called the noble path. Since it has eight steps, it is called the Noble Eightfold Path. One who follows the Noble Eightfold Path is called a noble disciple.

After he attained enlightenment, the Buddha went to Varanasi where he delivered his first sermon on the four most important truths he had realized, which are known as the Four Noble Truths. The first truth is that life is characterized by dissatisfaction or suffering. The second is that to abandon suffering, we must abandon the cause of suffering—primarily craving or greed, but also hatred, ignorance, and other delusions. The third is that suffering does have an end or cessation—nibbana—which arises when greed, hatred, and ignorance have been destroyed. And the fourth is the method required to reach this goal, following the Noble Eightfold Path. This path—right understanding, right thinking, right speaking, right action, right livelihood, right effort, right mindfulness, and right concentration—is the method through which we overcome existing defilements and cultivate noble qualities.

The method for attaining spiritual achievement laid out by the Buddha is not theoretical. Before he attained enlightenment, even the Buddha's mind was not totally pure. Like us, he was afflicted with psychic irritants—the three unwholesome roots, craving, hatred, and ignorance, and their offshoots, the hindrances and fetters. Hindrances are negative tendencies of mind. The Satipatthana Sutta lists five hindrances: sensory craving, restlessness and worry, ill will, laziness, and skeptical doubt. These negative states interfere with our ability to concentrate when we are meditating and thus block our spiritual progress. A hindrance appears temporarily and can be overcome by the application of effort.

The fetters are more durable and deeply rooted habits of the unenlightened mind. There are ten fetters: belief in a permanent self, skeptical doubt, clinging to rituals, sensory craving, hatred, craving for fine material existence, craving for immaterial existence, conceit, restlessness, and ignorance. These ten negative mental habits bind us to life after life in the cycle of suffering known as samsara. Though some of the fetters have the same names as the hindrances, the fetters are more deeply rooted in the mind. For this reason, it takes more effort and deeper levels of mindfulness and concentration to root them out. The fetters are like a bamboo shoot. Once a shoot takes hold, it quickly multiplies and grows into an enormous bush. Digging out the root is difficult, and unless every part of the root is removed, the bamboo will grow back again and again. A similar tendency of mind is described in the suttas: "Just as a tree, though cut down, sprouts up again if its roots remain uncut and firm, even so, until the craving that lies dormant is rooted out, suffering springs up again and again."

To follow the Buddha's path toward purity of mind, we begin the practice with a birds-eye view or superficial understanding of the Noble Eightfold Path. We pay mindful attention to our body, feelings, perceptions, thoughts, and consciousness. Mindful attention is attention without greed, hatred, and delusion. When hindrances arise, we use mindfulness to block them from entering the mind. As the hindrances are overcome, we experience the power of pure concentration. We use this concentration to dig deeper into our mental functioning to recognize and uproot the fetters.

Through this process we see how the path unfolds. Each time we practice the Noble Eightfold Path, our mind becomes a little bit clearer. However, until the practice is perfect, our mind will not become totally pure. As we practice, our understanding deepens. As the understanding deepens, we keep on practicing. Then one day, the Noble Eightfold Path becomes so clear in our mind that skeptical doubt about the path disappears and positive qualities such as the seven factors of enlightenment begin to grow within us.

The End of Perception

Moreover, as our experience in mindfulness meditation deepens, a similar process of directed mindfulness helps us to reach the high mental states on the Buddha's path known as the *jhanas*. The jhanas are deep, tranquil states of meditation, in which numerous wholesome mental factors work together in harmony. As we progress through these high meditative states, our perception is increasingly purified, until perception itself is abandoned. Briefly, the sequence can be described as follows:

▸ Secluded from sense pleasures and unwholesome mental states, we enter and dwell in the first jhana. The first jhana is a beautiful pleasant feeling that arises from having restrained negative states of mind. We are able to "sink into" a meditative subject such as loving-friendliness with applied and sustained thought and experience rapture and happiness born from seclusion. The perceptions of sensual desire, hatred, restlessness and worry, sleepiness and drowsiness, and doubt are abandoned by training and a new perception of delight is aroused in the mind through training.

▸ In the second jhana, we let go of applied thought and sustained thought, and the mind becomes calm. This state is characterized by internal confidence and unification of mind and is filled with rapture and bliss born of concentration. At this time, the true and subtle perception of joy and happiness born of seclusion in the first jhana vanish through training and a new true and subtle perception of rapture and bliss born of concentration is aroused through training.

▶ In the third jhana, rapture fades away, and we experience pure mindfulness coupled with equanimity or even-mindedness. The mind is clear and discerning.

▶ In the fourth jhana, we experience neither pleasure nor pain, neither happiness nor unhappiness. Instead the mind is suffused with a true and subtle perception of equanimity and mindfulness. Here the cultivation of the Noble Eightfold Path narrows down to the last step, right concentration. This powerful concentration perceives the impermanence, suffering, and selflessness of the five aggregates and comprehends this truth without thoughts or words. Concepts such as "I," or "mine," or "I am" vanish, and insight and tranquility take their place. Mind is luminous, pure, bright, and unblemished.

The fourth jhana profoundly changes our perception. As mind becomes increasingly pure, perception begins to reach its limits. Though a pleasant, unpleasant, or neutral feeling may still arise as a result of contact between the mind and a mental object, the cognition of these feelings occurs without clinging, aversion, or ignorance. We simply cognize the pleasant feeling, unpleasant feeling, or neutral feeling, while understanding at the same time that when contact with the mental object that caused this feeling ceases, the corresponding feeling will also subside and cease.

The mind remains in a state of equanimity—not grasping at pleasant perceptions, pushing away unpleasant ones, or ignoring neutral ones. We understand deeply that all perceptions and the objects that cause them to arise are impermanent—that there is no holding or delight in them, no pushing away or disgust in them, and nothing to ignore. The mind becomes like pure gold, purified and bright, malleable, wieldy, and radiant. As the Buddha described this state in the Dhatuvibhaga Sutta:

> Suppose, bhikkhu, a skilled goldsmith or his apprentice were to prepare a furnace, heat up the crucible, take some gold with tongs, and put it into the crucible. From time to time he would blow on it, from time to time he would sprinkle water over it, and from time to time he would just look on. That gold would become refined, well refined, completely refined, faultless, rid of dross, malleable, wieldy, and radiant. Then whatever kind of ornament he wished to make from it, whether a golden chain or earrings or a necklace or a golden garland, it would serve his purpose. So too, bhikkhu, [in the mind] then there remains only equanimity, purified and bright, malleable, wieldy, and radiant. (tr. Bhikkhu Bodhi)

Then, like a goldsmith working with purified metal, we apply our well trained mind to our meditation, which moves beyond the material sphere of the first four jhanas into the last four immaterial jhana states: the perception of infinite space, the perception of infinite consciousness, the perception of voidness, and neither perception nor nonperception. These states are called immaterial because we achieve them by overcoming all perceptions of material form. At each successive stage, former perceptions fade away and new, more purified perceptions arise, until the limit of perception is reached. At that point, we understand, "Mental activity is worse for me. Lack of mental activity is better. If I were to think and imagine, these pure perceptions that I have attained would cease, and coarser perceptions would arise in me. Suppose I were not to think or imagine?" So we neither think nor imagine.

Because only purified perceptions arise, coarser perceptions no longer arise. Equanimity is purified and bright. For this reason, we do not form positive or negative thoughts or feelings, nor do we generate any good or ill intentions toward people or things. For this reason, we do not cling to anything in this world comprised of our mind and body. When we do not cling, we are not agitated. When we are not agitated, we attain cessation—personal nibbana, the end of suffering. As the Buddha expressed the knowledge and vision that arises in this state: "Unshakable is the liberation of my mind. This is my last birth. Now there is no more renewed existence."

PART 2: TEN HEALING PERCEPTIONS

· 4 ·

PERCEPTION OF IMPERMANENCE

On one occasion the Blessed One was dwelling at Savatthi in Jeta's Grove, Anāthapindika's Park. Now on that occasion the Venerable Girimananda was sick, afflicted, and gravely ill.

Then the Venerable Ananda approached the Blessed One, paid homage to him, sat down to one side, and said to him:

"Bhante, the Venerable Girimananda is sick, afflicted, and gravely ill. It would be good if the Blessed One would visit him out of compassion."

"If, Ananda, you visit the bhikkhu Girimananda and speak to him about ten perceptions, it is possible that on hearing about them his affliction will immediately subside. What are the ten?

"(1) The perception of impermanence, (2) the perception of nonself, (3) the perception of unattractiveness, (4) the perception of danger, (5) the perception of abandoning, (6) the perception of dispassion, (7) the perception of cessation, (8) the perception of nondelight in the entire world, (9) the perception of impermanence in all conditioned phenomena, and (10) mindfulness of breathing." *(tr. Bhikkhu Bodhi)*

....

O UT OF MANY PERCEPTIONS, the Buddha selected ten as healing perceptions and requested the Venerable Ananda to relate them to Girimananda. Why did he select these ten? The apparent reason is that these perceptions are not distorted. Perhaps the Venerable Girimananda was ill because he was afflicted with distorted perceptions. To cure him, the Buddha wanted him to see the undistorted truth in each of the ten. Seeing the truth, the mind becomes delighted. The Buddha wanted to arouse joy in Girimananda by encouraging him to recognize and accept that everything is always changing. Knowing this, Girimananda would not cling. Not clinging to the body, mind, feelings, thoughts, or perceptions—the five aggregates—Girimananda would not suffer. As the Buddha said:

Fully knowing
The arising and passing of the aggregates,
One attains joy and delight,
For those who know, this is the deathless.

In this part, we look at each of the ten perceptions the Buddha mentioned for the benefit of Girimananda and examine how it can help to end suffering. Before we begin, it's important to understand the logic of the Buddha's healing method. The Buddha, who is often described as a "physician" or "surgeon," treated patients suffering from various physical and psychological ailments. The Dhamma medicine he prescribed often consisted of facing up to truths that people would rather avoid. We would rather hear that things are permanent, full of pleasure, and sustained and nourished by self. But when we are suffering, we are willing to go along with procedures that are unpleasant or painful. Even though we may be reluctant, we allow the physician's nurse to jab us with a syringe and draw blood to diagnose our sickness and then agree to take whatever medicine the doctor prescribes. In the same way, to achieve peace of mind, the Buddha was telling us, we must contemplate some painful truths.

So, for example, the Buddha recommended first of all meditation on the perception of impermanence. For a person proud of having lived a long life, he recommended reflecting on the inevitability of death. To avoid the grief and despair caused by attachment to loved ones, he recommended reflecting on the truth of suffering caused by separation from loved ones. Paradoxically, by contemplating impermanence, we begin our progress on the path toward permanent peace.

Then we meditate on the selflessness of everything that exists. To help us understand selflessness in practical terms, we meditate next on the dissatisfaction and suffering that comes along with having a body made up of many parts, all of which are aging and decaying and none of which contains anything that can be called a "self." When we realize deeply that the body and its parts are opportunities for suffering, including the pains of old age, illness, and death, we meditate on abandoning the causes of suffering—desire and craving. This realization spurs us to meditate on cultivating an attitude of dispassion or detachment toward the painful and pleasurable experiences of this life. Dispassion leads us to meditate on cessation, the Buddha's promise that suffering has an end. To achieve cessation, we meditate on giving up the last vestiges of craving, even craving for future rebirth. Finally, we meditate once again on mindfulness of breathing, the general method we must use to achieve each of the previous realizations.

Seen in this light, the Girimananda Sutta is a complete meditation program that promises to heal not only diseases of the body and mind but to move us forward toward the ultimate healing of liberation or nibbana.

....

"And what, Ananda, is the perception of impermanence? Here, having gone to the forest, to the foot of a tree, or to an empty hut, a bhikkhu reflects thus: 'Form is impermanent, feeling is impermanent, perception is impermanent, volitional activities are impermanent, consciousness is impermanent.' Thus he dwells contemplating impermanence in these five aggregates subject to clinging. This is called the perception of impermanence." *(tr. Bhikkhu Bodhi)*

The first healing perception is that the five aggregates—form, feeling or sensation, perception, thought or mental formations, and consciousness—are impermanent, always and inevitably changing. The Buddha was not alone in his time to recognize this truth. Contemporaries like the Greek philosopher Heraclitus also saw that everything is impermanent. Heraclitus said, "You cannot step into the same river twice." But we don't know what the ancient Greeks did with this understanding of impermanence. Mere theoretical knowledge of impermanence does not really help us or change anything. The knowledge must be experiential and it must be used for some good purpose.

Actually, recognizing impermanence is not very difficult. When I was in the Buddhist Vihara in Washington, D.C., the first Theravada Buddhist monastic community established in the United States, there was a baby boy only ten days old. His father brought him to the Vihara very often. This very tiny baby appeared to be very happy to see me. When he began to crawl, he crawled toward me and affectionately stretched his hands toward me to be lifted and carried. He grew up like my own child. One day, when he was almost ten years old, I returned to the Vihara from one of my trips. The child came to me and wanted to hug me. I told him, "You are so big now, you are unhuggable."

"Bhante," he agreed, "let us face facts. Everything is impermanent. I am grown up, and you cannot hug me any more."

Even this little boy knew that everything is impermanent!

We also acknowledge impermanence, but our acknowledgement is superficial. Deep in our subconscious, a sense of permanence is lurking. Perhaps this hidden sense is why we keep patching up our broken teeth, dry skin, brittle nails, gray hair, hunched backs, weak eyes, impaired hearing, breaking bones, and many other problems caused in this fragile body by impermanence. Similarly, our moods, feelings, thoughts, perceptions, and memories go through many changes each moment. We take medicines, see mental health specialists, and engage in many other activities, including meditation, to correct our minds. But while we are doing all this, impermanence is still going on, systematically altering and ultimately destroying everything inside our body and mind. Our organs, our cells, the nervous system, the quality of our blood, the strength of our lungs, and the very structure of our bones are all going through very rapid and unmistakable changes. No matter how much we patch up the surface, beneath the skin, impermanence is very consistently working its course. Nothing on earth—no science, no technology, no magic—can stop this change.

When we realize that this is the case, the question becomes, what should we do with this knowledge? How can we make our understanding useful? The Buddha's answer is that impermanence is the key that opens the mind to understanding suffering and nonself. He pointed out clearly the connection between impermanence and suffering. He taught that it is not impermanence itself that causes suffering but rather clinging to impermanent things. When we do not cling to impermanent things, our suffering ends. As the Buddha said in the Mahasunnata Sutta: "I do not see even a single kind of form, Ananda, from the change and alteration of which there would not arise sorrow, lamentation, pain, grief, and despair in one who lusts for it and takes delight in it."

This passage states clearly that suffering arises not because an object is impermanent but because we are attached to it. When we attain enlightenment, we do not suffer. But no impermanent thing has become permanent. Impermanent things continue to be impermanent whether we attain enlightenment or not. Nothing stops a thing's impermanent nature, which would exist whether or not the Buddhas had come into existence. Enlightenment ends suffering because enlightened beings do not lust for or take delight in things that are in every moment changing or passing away. Our suffering will also end when we give up our attachment to impermanent things.

But in his profound wisdom, the Buddha went a few steps further. He saw that not only is it impossible for a person to step into the same river twice, but the same person cannot step into a river twice. In other words, not only are things around us changing, but we ourselves are changing every moment as well. When we meditate on the five aggregates of our own body and mind, we can see that all of them—past, present, or future, internal or external, gross or subtle, low or high, far or near—are impermanent, changing and fading away without leaving behind any trace of their existence. Nothing is imperishable. Nothing stays forever. Everything disappears without leaving behind any sign of its existence. This understanding is called "signlessness." As the Buddha said in the Khandavagga:

> Form is like a lump of foam,
> Feeling like a water bubble;
> Perception is like a mirage,
> Volitions like a plantain trunk,
> And consciousness like an illusion.
> (tr. Bhikkhu Bodhi)

Awareness of signlessness helps to evaporate our clinging desire for anything impermanent. It also evaporates our hatred or resentment, since there is nothing permanent for us to hate or resent. The very desire to hang on to anything ends up in frustration causing suffer-ing. Contemplation of this suffering arouses wishless liberation. Our ordinary human "wish list" is exhausted. There is no more yearning for anything. This understanding is called "wishlessness." Because everything is disappearing without leaving any trace behind, there also arises in us the awareness of selflessness. There is nothing and no one to hold. There is no core, nor is there any immovable mover. The very notion of self evaporates. This understanding is called "selfless-ness" or "emptiness."

Wishlessness, along with signlessness and emptiness, are often called the "three gateways to liberation." When we recognize that every impermanent thing is changing and leaves no trace, and that every sign-less, impermanent thing is empty of self and leads only to suffering, our desire to possess or hold on to ever-changing, suffering-producing, and selfless things and people evaporates. We wish only to be liberated—to be free from all of it. As the Buddha explained, "Seeing thus, the impermanence, suffering, and selflessness of all conditioned things, one becomes disenchanted with everything."

Because of this disenchantment, we become dispassionate, which means that we do not wish for anything and do not cling. With a dispassionate mind, we are able to see the cessation, or ending, of everything—even life itself—with calmness and equanimity. This wis-dom causes us to let go of attachment once and for all. In this way, we develop insight into the nature of reality. Our life becomes, the Bud-dha said, like the untraceable path of the birds in the sky. All notions of permanence, any sign of greed, and any notion of self vanish from the mind. All that remains is freedom. As the Dhammapada says:

Like the path of birds in the sky
It is hard to trace the path

Of those who do not hoard
Who are judicious with their food,
And whose field
Is the freedom of emptiness and signlessness.
(tr. Gil Fronsdal)

Here we must remember that disenchantment does not mean anything negative. It is the positive and mature attitude of someone who has grown into spiritual adulthood. The Buddha used a very meaningful analogy to explain what he meant by disenchantment. Imagine that some children are making sandcastles on the beach. While building the castles and playing with them, the children imagine that the castles are real. Adults who are watching the children play with the castles are amused, reflecting on the nature of the children's minds. Unlike the children, they do not engage in make believe or pretend that the castles are real. After a while, the children become disappointed and grow tired of playing with the castles. They stop pretending, destroy the castles, and scatter the sand here and there. Since they did not pretend that the castles were real, the adults are not disappointed with the castles' destruction.

Like the children, the Buddha said, we are often playing pretend games with impermanent sandcastles. But eventually, we begin to see that attachment to impermanent things, especially the five aggregates, causes suffering to arise. Because things are changing without prior notice, dissatisfaction arises. Since impermanence applies to us as well as to everything around us, we come to realize that there is no permanent self or soul and nothing that can control or stop the process of disintegration. Seeing this entire process with wisdom, we become disenchanted with everything conditioned by suffering and impermanence. Seeing impermanence with wisdom is the key to abandoning unwholesome habits of body and mind. It helps us to cultivate an attitude of nonattachment to conditioned things, and ultimately, it leads us to the cessation of suffering.

Moreover, as we learn in the Girimananda Sutta, perception of impermanence can help to cure sickness. How impermanence heals is not difficult to understand. Impermanence does not exist in a vacuum. There must be something there in the first place to be impermanent. The five aggregates of body, feelings, perceptions, thoughts, and consciousness are impermanent. Within consciousness, contact and attention are impermanent. As we said, contact, feelings, perceptions, thoughts, and attention are factors of the mind that occur whenever the senses come into contact with an object. All of these elements of mental functioning are impermanent.

When we are ill or experience bodily pain, sometimes the mind grows depressed. But knowing impermanence, we perceive that our illness and the pain it causes are also changing all the time. So instead of complaining, we pay attention to the changes taking place. When we pay attention with mindfulness, we notice that our pain sometimes increases and sometimes decreases. As we watch with mindfulness, we might even forget the painful feeling and watch with dispassion as the painful feeling fades away and a neutral feeling arises. As it does, we also notice that our feeling of mental depression fades away and is replaced by a neutral feeling.

Being mindful of these changes, sometimes the impermanence of the painful feelings leads to a feeling of happiness arising because we can see the gradual disappearance of our impermanent pain! With this realization, we become full of joy, and delightful feelings arise. Delightful feelings are always positive. They release healthy chemicals in the body and mind. These healthy chemicals accelerate the healing process. In this way, healing follows from our perception of the truth of the impermanence of painful feelings. Thus perception of impermanence can lead both to healing the pains of this life and, ultimately, to full liberation from the cycle of suffering—nibbana.

· 5 ·

PERCEPTION OF SELFLESSNESS

"And what, Ananda, is the perception of non-self? Here, having gone to the forest, to the foot of a tree, or to an empty hut, a bhikkhu reflects thus: 'The eye is nonself, forms are nonself; the ear is nonself, sounds are nonself; the nose is nonself, odors are nonself; the tongue is nonself, tastes are nonself; the body is nonself, tactile objects are nonself; the mind is nonself, mental phenomena are nonself.' Thus he dwells contemplating nonself in these six internal and external sense bases. This is called the perception of nonself." (*tr. Bhikkhu Bodhi*)

....

As the Buddha explained in this passage, the six sense organs, their external objects or "tactile objects" and internal objects or "mental phenomena," as well as the mind and body are all absent of self. In our mindfulness meditation, we examine each in turn and are forced to conclude that all things—past, present, or future, interior or exterior, gross or subtle—are impermanent and unsatisfactory. Moreover, there is no power that can make the impermanent permanent and the unsatisfactory satisfactory.

When we see things correctly and with wisdom, we can say conclusively regarding everything that exists, "this is not mine," "this I am not," and "this is not myself." Of course, for convenience in our everyday lives, we might say, "I am here" or "this belongs to me." But we must not fool ourselves into thinking that these words imply that there is any unchanging entity at all that I am or that belongs to me. Rather, as our perception of impermanence demonstrates, everything is in continual flux and flow, building up and breaking down according to ever-changing causes and conditions. Of course, this perpetual change applies as well to the five aggregates of the mind and body—form, feelings, thoughts, perceptions, and consciousness. Precisely because these aspects of mind and body are always changing, there is nothing within us that we can identify as a permanent self or soul.

The doctrine of selflessness, which is unique to the Buddha's teaching, has several important implications. For one thing, it counters the belief that life comes into being as a result of a creator god from whom the self or soul comes into existence and to whom the self or soul returns when life ends. Some people may be dismayed by the loss of the certainty provided by the doctrine of a creator god and argue that without such certainty, life is meaningless or hopeless. However, adhering to notions of permanence and certainty can encourage people to act in ways that are rigid and inflexible. Accepting the doctrine of selflessness, on the other hand, helps us to feel more relaxed and contented with whatever occurs, since we know that both pleasant and unpleasant experiences are temporary conditions. We understand that the absence of certainty gives us the opportunity to adapt to changing circumstances and, as spiritual adults, to assume responsibility for our own lives.

Moreover, the perception of selflessness helps to cure sickness, as is demonstrated in many suttas. In the Khemaka Sutta, we hear the story of Venerable Khemaka, a follower of the Buddha who was diseased, in pain, and severely ill. Several elders of the Buddha's community went to Khemaka and questioned him about the Buddha's doctrine of selflessness. While explaining the meaning of nonself, the Venerable Khemaka and the monks who listened to his explanation all attained enlightenment.

The reason that perception of selflessness has the power to heal can be understood in this way: While explaining the meaning of nonself, the Venerable Khemaka was very calm and relaxed. The elders in his audience were also very calm and relaxed. Letting go of anxiety and tension is a great healing remedy psychologically and physically. We have all experienced how stress and anxiety increases the pain we experience when we are ill. For instance, when we are waiting for a diagnosis from the doctor, our painful symptoms are often made worse because of imagination and fear. When we learn that our illness can be cured, we relax and our pain often decreases. Similarly, when someone listens very mindfully to an explanation of nonself, they are relieved of the tension and pressure that comes from thinking that there is a self that they need to protect. When we relax the mind and let go of this tension and pressure, we give tremendous relief to the mind and body. This relief is a very powerful means of releasing positive energy to accelerate the healing process.

In the case of the Venerable Girimananda, we might surmise that his illness was related to rigidity and tension caused by holding distorted views regarding the self. The Buddha as physician properly diagnosed this problem and gave Girimananda the correct medicine. Contemplating the perception of selflessness, Girimananda was able to relax enough to accelerate his recovery and regain his health.

· 6 ·

PERCEPTION OF IMPURITIES

"And what, Ananda, is the perception of unattractiveness? Here, a bhikkhu reviews this very body upward from the soles of the feet and downward from the tips of the hairs, enclosed in skin, as full of many kinds of
impurities: 'There are in this body hair of the head, hair of the body, nails,
teeth, skin, flesh, sinews, bones, bone marrow, kidneys, heart, liver, pleura,
spleen, lungs, intestines, mesentery, stomach, excrement, bile, phlegm,
pus, blood, sweat, fat, tears, grease, saliva, snot, fluid of the joints, urine.'
Thus he dwells contemplating unattractiveness in this body. This is called
the perception of unattractiveness." (*tr. Bhikkhu Bodhi*)

....

ANOTHER WAY OF SAYING "unattractiveness", which I prefer to
use here, is "impurity." Perception of the impurity of the various
parts of the body is an important part of meditation on perception.
When we look at ourselves in the mirror, we feel proud if the body
looks beautiful or displeased if the body seems unattractive. Perception of impurity teaches us to perceive the body realistically, exactly
as it is, without distortion and without the emotional reactions of
attachment and aversion that we normally feel. The key to perceiving
the body and its parts correctly is mindfulness. What our reflection in
the mirror does not show is that the body and its parts are impermanent, unsatisfactory, and selfless. But when we examine the body with
mindful attention, we see these dhamma qualities arising from each

part. "Impurity" in this context does not mean that parts of the body are unpleasant, though some clearly are. Rather, it points to the truth that the body and its parts are always changing and, in fact, decaying, and for that reason, the body is unsatisfactory and lacks any permanent self or soul.

Learning to look at the body realistically and with wisdom is very important to our psychological health. We all know people who are obsessively proud of their attractive appearance and others who are depressed because they perceive themselves to be unattractive according to their own whims and fancies. Through meditating on the impurity of the body, we are reconditioning ourselves to perceive the parts of the body as they are without attaching to anything or rejecting anything. This perception, which goes against the grain of our normal way of perceiving, brings tremendous relief to the mind. When we perceive something exactly as it is, we do not love it nor do we hate it. Instead, we let go of our conceptions of beauty and ugliness and perceive the body as simply impermanent, suffering, and selfless.

The attitude we are seeking to cultivate about the body and its parts is equanimity. In the Satipaṭṭhana Sutta, the Buddha gave a helpful illustration of this essential attitude. Suppose, the Buddha said, there is a bag full of grain—rice, hill rice, paddy rice, lentils, barley, sesame seeds, mustard seeds, peas, and others. Let's say that there are thirty-two kinds of seeds inside the bag. We open the bag and ask a man with good eyesight to look inside. The person looking into the bag might say, "There is rice, hill rice, paddy rice, lentils, barley, sesame seeds, mustard seeds, and peas." He simply recognizes and identifies the various seeds. He does not say, "This is barley; I hate barley." Or "This is sesame seed; I love sesame seeds." He just recognizes the grains exactly as they are. That is mindful recognition, recognition with equanimity.

We can easily see how such realistic perception can help to heal illness. When he was sick, the Venerable Girimananda may have felt attachment to parts of the body that he perceived as healthy and hatred toward parts that he perceived as diseased. Diagnosing this condition correctly, the Buddha tactfully taught Girimananda to perceive his body parts impartially. Meditating on the various parts of his own body, Girimananda realized that every part is fragile and subject to affliction. There was no reason for him to feel attachment or aversion to any part. This even-minded and balanced perception gave him psychological and physical relief and helped his body to heal.

Since meditation on the impurity of parts of the body is so important and so helpful, let's consider in more detail how we can get started with practicing this meditation.

- ▶ First, we catalog the various parts of the body so that we can focus our perception. The Buddha divided the body into thirty-two parts, as mentioned in the sutta. The first twenty of these parts are solid and belong to the body's earth element. The last twelve parts are liquid and belong to the body's water element.

- ▶ We begin our meditation by considering the first five solid parts: head-hairs, body-hairs, nails, teeth, and skin. We start with these five because they are the most visible parts and the parts that our eyes catch when we first meet a person. They are also the parts that many people decorate, paint, and shape in many ways to attract others toward them. Because these parts are so prominent, meditators can easily use them to gain insight into how they perceive the physical body. True, deep understanding of these five visible parts helps us to reflect upon many other invisible parts inside the skin.

- ▶ For example, hair on the head is a very powerful subject for meditation. We remember that ordinarily, the hair is considered to be an object of beauty. In ancient Indian tradition, long hair is one of the five attractive qualities of a woman. In Western culture as well, people spend a lot of money on their hair. Hair care specialists invent many products to enhance the hair. The media is full of advertisements for these products, promising they will make hair good looking, natural looking, beautiful looking, healthy looking, young looking, attractive, and long lasting. A new haircut is often a topic for group discussion. If a man's hair begins to fall out, he will often spend time and money trying to reverse or disguise his baldness.

▸ But looking at the hair on the head with mindfulness, we can see that our hair is actually more like a garbage can. Dandruff, dust, dead skin, and even lice can accumulate on the head. When it is unwashed for one or two days, the hair begins to smell and grow oily. We try to keep the hair very clean all the time. We shampoo it, curl or straighten it, and comb it daily. How our hair looks plays a big part in determining whether we feel attractive or unattractive. Mindfulness of the effort we put into caring for our hair helps us to recognize the real truth of the situation.

▸ Mindfulness also reveals how impermanent hair is. Perhaps we remember that many years ago when we were young, our hair was soft, healthy, and smooth. As we grow older, it goes from rich brown, black, red, or blonde to gray or white. It becomes brittle. It thins or falls out completely. This is impermanence.

▸ We also realize that hair is actually not a very pleasant thing. We admire the hair while it is on our head, but if one of those beautiful and admirable hairs falls into our bowl of soup, we may throw the entire bowl of soup away! Hair that once gave us pleasure and joy now brings us displeasure and sadness. From this example, we see that hair is also unsatisfactory.

▶ Finally, we recognize that hair is not the self. It is not permanent and cannot give us lasting satisfaction. We have no control over what happens to our hair or any other part of the body because it is not the self.

▶ As a result of this meditation, we conclude, "This hair on the head is not mine; it is not 'I' and not my 'self'." It is as impermanent and unsatisfactory as anything else in this body and mind.

▶ When we mindfully perceive the hair on the head and cultivate equanimity about this part of the body, it doesn't matter whether the hair is on the head or in a bowl of soup. Our attitude toward it is the same.

Once we have cultivated balance and equanimity about our hair, we meditate on each of the other parts as well. Whether the part is something that we consider beautiful and admirable or something we consider disgusting and repulsive, we try to cultivate a similar attitude towards it. Our aim is not to feel disgust at the body but rather to perceive a part of the body as it is without distortions or imposed concepts, such as the notions that the body is beautiful, or that it is the source of happiness, or that it is permanent, or that it has a permanent soul in it. We look at each part of the body, visible or invisible, with the wisdom that sees that this body, like everything else that exists, is neither beautiful nor ugly. Instead, it is a thing composed of many parts all of which are subject to an ever-changing process. This is called "seeing the body with the wisdom of equanimity." When we accept the body exactly as it is, we feed the body, clean the body, put the body to sleep, and take care of the body exactly as we normally do, yet we do all this with realistic understanding that is free of delusion or distortion.

Meditating mindfully on the parts of the body also helps us understand a deeper truth. Since every part of the body that we examine with mindfulness is shown to be impermanent and in fact decaying, we are able to recognize and acknowledge that no matter how handsome, beautiful, young, healthy, or strong we feel, eventually we will grow old and lose our handsomeness, beauty, youth, health, and strength. Because we are also training ourselves to view these changes with equanimity, recognizing that the body and its parts are not my "self," we are no longer so fearful when we perceive our body going through these inevitable changes. When we relinquish attachment to our body, our suffering decreases and our mind becomes calm.

Knowledge of the true nature of the parts of the body also helps us to take care of the body without anxiety when things go wrong. Seeing the body's parts exactly as they are—changing, weakening, falling ill, returning to health—helps us to use attention, concentration, and visualization to cultivate strong willpower so that when we do get sick, we can use the mind to generate positive substances that affect overall body chemistry. Sometimes it is possible to focus our mind on a defective part with a strong power of visualization and accelerate its healing. However, when we diligently understand the body and its parts, we are not overly emotional or upset if healing does not occur and remain calm even at the thought of death.

· 7 ·

PERCEPTION OF DANGER

"And what, Ananda, is the perception of danger? Here, having gone to the forest, to the foot of a tree, or to an empty hut, a bhikkhu reflects thus: 'This body is the source of much pain and danger; for all sorts of afflictions arise in this body, that is, eye-disease, disease of the inner ear, nose-disease, tongue-disease, body-disease, head-disease, disease of the external ear, mouth-disease, tooth-disease, cough, asthma, catarrh, pyrexia, fever, stomachache, fainting, dysentery, gripes, cholera, leprosy, boils, eczema, tuberculosis, epilepsy, ringworm, itch, scab, chickenpox, scabies, hemorrhage, diabetes, hemorrhoids, cancer, fistula; illnesses originating from bile, phlegm, wind, or their combination; illnesses produced by change of climate; illnesses produced by careless behavior; illnesses produced by assault; or illnesses produced as the result of kamma; and cold, heat, hunger, thirst, defecation, and urination.' Thus he dwells contemplating danger in this body. This is called the perception of danger." (tr. Bhikkhu Bodhi)

....

THIS SECTION of the Girimananda Sutta lists various illnesses human beings may experience. The Buddha mentioned forty-eight different kinds of illness, which arise from eight causes: wind, bile, phlegm, the union of the humors of the body (wind, bile, and phlegm), changes of seasons, abuse of the body, self-mutilation, and kamma. As we read through the Buddha's list, we recognize that many of these same diseases trouble us today. Though our understanding of the causes of illness may be more sophisticated than it was in the Buddha's time, we experience the same problems because the human body and its parts are still impermanent, subject to suffering, and selfless, as the Buddha taught.

Why did the Buddha list these diseases, and what do we learn by reading through this list? Traditionally, five explanations are given. First, the list reminds us of the imperfections of the aggregate of form. It illustrates that this body, whose health we guard so carefully, is made up of parts, each of which is subject to breaking down in a number of ways. This perception challenges the comfortable notion that the body is a single entity that is strong, healthy, beautiful, or enduring. It helps us remember how vulnerable we are and how often and in how many ways the impermanent form aggregate can lead to pain and suffering. Second, as we read through this catalog of illnesses and their causes, we are reminded that illness is an everyday occurrence in the reality of human life. Our goal in contemplating these diseases is to accept this reality with full awareness, while avoiding emotional reactions such as craving and fear that illness often provokes.

Third, reading this list reminds us again that the body is impermanent. While we are reading this paragraph, every cell, organ, and system of our body is changing—growing, decaying, or dying. The heart is beating; the lungs are circulating air; the kidneys, liver, and stomach are performing their functions. Nothing is solid or reliable. Distress or disease of some kind is always possible and, in fact, inevitable. Recognizing this truth lessens the pain of illness when it arises. Fourth, remembering that illness is always a possibility helps us to avoid feelings of pride when we are enjoying good health and of condescending pity for those who are sick. Finally, the list encourages us to take precautions and make changes in our behavior to avoid experiencing these painful conditions. For example, in other suttas, the Buddha recommends eating a light diet as a way to help maintain the body's health.

Many suttas describe the Buddha as a physician and surgeon. In his wisdom, he was able to diagnose the nature of an illness and prescribe appropriate treatment. Generally, the Buddha's prescription was not medicine in the traditional sense but the potent elixir of Dhamma that has the power to heal misperceptions in the mind and banish pain and disease once and for all. As the Buddha said in a sutta:

> Of all the medicines in the world,
> Manifold and various,
> There is none like the medicine of Dhamma.
> Therefore, O monks, drink of this.
> Having drunk this Dhamma medicine,
> You will be ageless and beyond death;
> Having developed and seen the truth,
> You will be quenched, free from craving.

Being free from craving is potent medicine. Worry, stress, nervous breakdowns, depression, addiction, quarrels, and even divorce all arise because of the negative emotions of attachment and anger. Physical illness as well is strongly linked to our emotional health. For instance, when we allow ourselves to be constantly irritated, eventually we get angry. Unchecked anger becomes hatred. When we are full of hate, we do not sleep well. Lack of sleep raises our blood pressure, which can lead in turn to a stroke or heart attack. Conversely, when the mind is calm and relaxed, we get sick less frequently, suffer less when we do, and heal more quickly.

Knowing this, the Buddha prescribed perception of danger as part of Girimananda's treatment. Whatever physical ailment Girimananda was experiencing, the medicine of the Dhamma was an appropriate cure. Not only could the Dhamma alleviate Girimananda's emotional and physical suffering, but it could also lead him to nibbana, which is ageless and beyond death. This is how the knowledge of truth becomes medicine.

· 8 ·

PERCEPTION OF ABANDONING

"And what, Ananda, is the perception of abandoning? Here, a bhikkhu does not tolerate an arisen sensual thought; he abandons it, dispels it, terminates it, and obliterates it. He does not tolerate an arisen thought of ill will . . . an arisen thought of harming . . . bad unwholesome states whenever they arise; he abandons them, dispels them, terminates them, and obliterates them. This is called the perception of abandoning." (*tr. Bhikkhu Bodhi*)

ABANDONING IS GIVING UP or getting rid of something. In this section, the Buddha is counseling Girimananda to abandon, dispel, and get rid of thoughts of sensuous pleasure, hatred, hurting others, and any other unwholesome or unskillful ideas and impulses. The perception of abandoning is not passive. Our tendency to engage in thoughts of pleasure, in hateful or hurtful thoughts, and in many other unskillful thoughts such as pride, jealousy, and stinginess is deeply rooted in the mind. The perception of abandoning requires vigilant effort to watch the mind so that we can intervene if such thoughts arise. As we have said, thought always precedes action. Our task is to use mindfulness to nip harmful thoughts in the bud before they have the opportunity to ripen into unwholesome actions.

Before he attained enlightenment, the Buddha divided his thoughts into two categories: unwholesome and wholesome. The first category included thoughts of attachment, hatred, and harming others. When he noticed that any of these thoughts were arising in his mind, he reflected on the negative consequences to himself and to others of entertaining it. Then he took conscious steps to abandon it. When that particular negative thought had been overcome, he maintained his mindfulness to keep other unwholesome thoughts from arising.

For instance, the Buddha knew that attachment to sensuous pleasure brings very little true happiness and actually causes much suffering. Because of the pleasure they experience, unenlightened people are temporarily blinded to the consequences of sensuous indulgence and give in to impulses toward attachment. In everyday experience, we frequently experience this short-circuiting of our nobler impulses. Though we may accept intellectually that "love is blind," only after we have endured the suffering of an unhappy attachment do we remember this common expression. When we are in love, we often tell ourselves that the rest of the world is blind and that only we can see the true value of the object of our attachment. But when we reflect on the pain that blind love causes, we realize that the very nature of sensuous desire is to make the mind excited, restless, and agitated. While desire dominates, the mind cannot be calm. Seeing this reality, the Buddha advised us to let go of sensual desire so that the mind can remain centered and peaceful.

In a similar way, thoughts of hatred disturb the mind. Hatred cannot make us happy. By entertaining thoughts of hatred, we actually create our own misery and perpetuate our suffering. We should not suffer foolishly. Especially when we are sick, we must use mindfulness to avoid developing hatred for the body or its infirmity. Unhappy emotions and negative states of mind actually aggravate our sickness. Getting rid of hatred, on the other hand, accelerates healing. Knowing this well, the Buddha advised Girimananda to refuse to tolerate hatred and get rid of it completely.

Even the thought of hurting others can hurt us. When we think carefully, we recognize that thoughts of harming actually hurt us and no one else. They are like rust that forms within an iron rod that eventually destroys the strength and integrity of the iron. In the same way, thoughts of harming others are like a cancer that grows inside the body and destroys its health and strength. In other words, when we abandon thoughts of harming others, we are also helping ourselves. We help immediately in that we experience less agitation and unhappiness and also ultimately in that we overcome the impulse to act in an unkind or hurtful way and thus avoid generating negative kamma.

One of the methods the Buddha recommended for overcoming negative thoughts is redirecting the mind toward thoughts that are beneficial. For instance, we replace thoughts of attachment to sensuous pleasure with thoughts of renunciation. Renunciation in this context is the same as abandoning or letting go. It is the conscious decision to let go of perceptions of desire, lust, greed, clinging, and craving. It is the conscious decision to restrain the senses to avoid disturbing impulses and refocus our attention on the goal of making the mind peaceful, relaxed, and serene.

Similarly, we work to abandon thoughts of hatred by replacing them with thoughts of loving-friendliness. We remember how agitated hatred makes us feel and how friendliness toward everyone and everything calms the mind and makes us happy. Loving-friendliness is also a natural impulse. When we abandon thoughts of hatred, loving-friendliness arises naturally to fill the void. When we no longer push things away, we feel friendly acceptance toward everything that exists, even toward our own body and illness.

The third beneficial thought is noncruelty. When thoughts of harming people or animals arise, we reflect on times when we have been treated badly and remember how much suffering harmful actions can cause. As a result, we replace thoughts of harming with thoughts of restraint and with compassion and care for others. Abandoning harmful thoughts helps to make us feel peaceful and happy, which helps us overcome our own suffering.

· 9 ·

PERCEPTION OF DISPASSION

"And what, Ananda, is the perception of dispassion? Here, having gone to
the forest, to the root of a tree, or to an empty hut, a bhikkhu reflects
thus: 'This is peaceful, this is sublime, that is, the stilling of all activities, the
relinquishment of all acquisitions, the destruction of craving, dispassion,
nibbāna.' This is called the perception of dispassion." (*tr. Bhikkhu Bodhi*)

....

DISPASSION IS the opposite of craving. As the realization
dawns that attachment to impermanent things causes suffering,
we become disenchanted with the desire to glue ourselves to pleasant feelings. Similarly, we recognize that our tendency to push away
unpleasant feelings is also craving—craving for conditions to be different than they actually are. Since conditions are always in flux, we
understand that feelings of aversion are also impermanent and become
disenchanted with them as well. Each time the mind tries to cling to
one thing and reject another, we discover that it is actually impossible
to cling to anything, because everything is changing all the time. Craving, we realize, is like trying to balance a mustard seed on the tip of a
moving needle.

In one of his early discourses, the Buddha explained why ending craving is so important. Several months after attaining enlightenment, the
Buddha was living at Gaya. On one occasion, he spoke to an audience of
one thousand ascetic monks who had been practicing fire worship. To

convey his message skillfully to this audience, he used the metaphor of fire. This teaching, known as "The Fire Sermon," explains the meaning of dispassion and why clinging of any kind must be ended. The only way to escape the fires that devour us, the Buddha said, is to extinguish them at their source. That source is perception itself. As the Buddha told the monks:

> Bhikkhus, all is burning. And what, bhikkhus, is the all that is burning? The eye is burning, forms are burning, eye-consciousness is burning, eye-contact is burning, and whatever feeling arises with eye-contact as condition— whether pleasant or painful or neither-painful-nor-pleasant—that too is burning. Burning with what? Burning with the fire of lust, with the fire of hatred, with the fire of delusion; burning with birth, aging, and death; with sorrow, lamentation, pain, displeasure, and despair, I say. (tr. Bhikkhu Bodhi)

The same is true, the Buddha continued, of the ear and sounds, the nose and smells, the tongue and tastes, the body and tactile sensations, and the mind and thoughts. In short, all six senses and their perceptual objects burn us with the fires of attachment, hatred, and delusion and lead to the repeated sufferings of birth, aging, illness, and death. Recognizing this truth:

> Seeing thus, bhikkhus, the instructed noble disciple experiences revulsion toward the eye, toward forms, toward eye-consciousness, toward eye-contact, toward whatever feeling arises with eye-contact as condition—whether pleasant or painful or neither-painful-nor-pleasant [. . .] experiencing revulsion, he becomes dispassionate. (tr. Bhikkhu Bodhi)

In this same way, we become disenchanted with all experiences of a sensual nature.

When a visual object appears, the mind rejects it with as little effort as closing our eyes or looking away from an object we don't want to see. When a sound strikes our ears, the mind lets go of it as quickly as we can snap our fingers. When smell touches our nose, the mind lets go of it as quickly as a drop of water rolls down a lotus leaf. When we touch something, the mind lets go of the sensation as easily as a strong man stretches his flexed arm or flexes his stretched arm. When a mental object appears in the mind, the mind lets go of it as quickly as drops of water evaporate when dropped into a frying pan that has been heating up all day.

Disenchanted with all sensory experiences, the Buddha said, we become dispassionate. Dispassion is the attitude that lacks interest in something. It causes us to turn away, especially from sensuous stimulation. Through dispassion, we let go of our habitual pattern of clinging to objects or experiences. When this attitude arises naturally as a result of our meditative development, we are released from suffering. According to the sutta, the one thousand monks who listened to the Buddha's Fire Sermon ended their clinging and attained nibbana, complete freedom from suffering.

The Buddha prescribed this portion of the sutta for Girimananda to direct his mind toward the unconditioned, nibbana. Nibbana is called "unconditioned" because in this perfect state, the mind is at peace, beyond being conditioned or affected by changes. In Nibbana, all suffering, including the discomfort of illness such as Girimananda was experiencing, is ended forever. For this reason, the Buddha was urging Girimananda—and us as well—to develop such strong mindfulness of dispassion that the mind does not cling to anything.

· 10 ·

PERCEPTION OF CESSATION

"And what, Ananda, is the perception of cessation? Here, having gone to the forest, to the root of a tree, or to an empty hut, a bhikkhu reflects thus: 'This is peaceful, this is sublime, that is, the stilling of all activities, the relinquishment of all acquisitions, the destruction of craving, cessation, nibbāna.' This is called the perception of cessation." (*tr. Bhikkhu Bodhi*)

WHEN WE TURN to the seventh perception, cessation, the first thing we notice is that the Buddha's description of this perception is nearly identical to his description of the perception of dispassion. The difference is that the word "dispassion" has been replaced by "cessation." This similarity of language tells us that as our mindfulness deepens, our cultivation of dispassion leads us toward perception of cessation. *Cessation* means "ending." It is the Buddha's promise that by following the path he laid out, our suffering will end once and for all.

In our current state of mind, it is almost impossible for us to comprehend what cessation might be like. Cessation arises only when we have succeeded in eliminating all negative states of mind—every kind of desire and hatred, as well as every kind of delusion or ignorance about the self. In other words, cessation is defined by what is not there. It arises only when we have put out the fires that arise from contact between our six perceptual senses and their objects. We may get a glimpse of cessation when we meditate with mindfulness that is so powerful that our deluded states of mind—what we earlier called the hindrances—have been eliminated. But we will not experience actual cessation until we reach the final stage of the Buddha's path.

As we progress through the stages of mindfulness meditation, from our earliest efforts to concentrate on the breath through the higher mental states called the jhanas, perception provides important mileposts. The Buddha made this point clearly in the Jhana Sutta: "Thus, I declare, Bhikkhus, that just so far as your perception-attainment goes, just so far your attainment of full enlightenment goes." In other words, our progress on the path toward cessation of suffering can be measured by the change in our understanding of and relationship to perception. By this point in our discussion, we can begin to appreciate the profound meaning of the Buddha's words. In the earlier stages of the path, contact between the six senses and their sensory objects was a distraction that hindered our ability to concentrate. Moreover, we regarded the objects of the senses, including the parts of our own body, as solid, enduring, and capable of bringing lasting pleasure or pain to "myself."

But as we meditate one by one on the ten perceptions, the mind gradually becomes convinced that nothing is enduring or pure, nothing can bring us lasting pleasure or pain, and nothing contains a permanent self or soul. Because of this understanding, our attention shifts from sensory perception and its objects to appreciation of the joys of seclusion and deep concentration. As the Buddha described this change in the Jhana Sutta:

> Here, secluded from sensual pleasures . . . a bhikkhu enters and dwells in the first jhāna . . . He considers whatever phenomena exist there pertaining to form, feeling, perception, volitional activities, and consciousness as impermanent, suffering, an illness, a boil, a dart, misery, affliction, alien,

disintegrating, empty, and nonself. He turns his mind away from those phenomena and directs it to the deathless element. (tr. Bhikkhu Bodhi)

In other words, starting in the first jhana, we recognize that our own aggregates—form, feeling, perception, fabrications [thoughts], and consciousness—are inconstant, suffering, sick, dangerous, afflictive, destructive, empty, and selfless. Having seen the aggregates in this light, we gradually turn our mind toward the opposite—nibbana and its cessation of all suffering. As the Buddha described this state beyond suffering in the Jhana Sutta:

> This is peaceful, this is sublime, that is, the stilling of all activities, the relinquishing of all acquisitions, the destruction of craving, dispassion, cessation, nibbāna. (tr. Bhikkhu Bodhi)

With our goal now clearly established, we enter jhana meditation again and again, using its pure, clear, and refined qualities of mind to end all conceptual thought and perception of conditioned phenomena. The exquisite tranquility of this peaceful state moves us beyond the desire for ordinary pleasure, ordinary good health, and even ordinary rebirth. As the Girimananda Sutta explains it: All "activities," including ideas of pleasure and pain, sickness and health, even life and death, are stilled, and we relinquish all craving, even the wish for "all acquisitions," including the most exalted rebirth. Instead we turn our mind toward the deathless joys of "cessation, nibbāna." As the Buddha reminded Girimananda at this point in the sutta, the promise of cessation motivates us to intensify our meditative efforts toward the attainment of these calm and excellent pleasures.

· 11 ·

PERCEPTION OF NONDELIGHT
IN THE WHOLE WORLD

"And what, Ananda, is the perception of nondelight in the entire world? Here, a bhikkhu refrains from any engagement and clinging, mental standpoints, adherences, and underlying tendencies in regard to the world, abandoning them without clinging to them. This is called the perception of nondelight in the entire world." (*tr. Bhikkhu Bodhi*)

....

THE PERCEPTION of nondelight in the whole world is difficult for us to understand right now. Usually, we do everything we can to increase our sense of delight in the life we have. However, by this time in our meditation on the ten perceptions, we have succeeded in convincing the mind that pleasurable worldly experiences are deceptive and, in fact, undesirable. They distract us from being able to concentrate and encourage grasping, aversion, and confusion. Moreover, we have begun to experience the peace and tranquility that come from abandoning sensory pleasure. We prefer the quieter and more intense inner joys of dispassion. As a result, it is relatively easy for us to give up delight in the ordinary world.

As we discover, the mind purified of greed, hatred, and delusion is naturally free from excitement when perceiving anything in the world. There is nothing special in the entire world for such a mind to delight in. Nor is there anything to be disappointed by. Nothing is extraordinary. The same problems of impermanence, suffering, and selflessness exist everywhere. Recognizing this truth, the mind becomes relaxed, peaceful, and calm.

But at a deeper level, we might hold out hope that some other life might be better than this one. Perhaps, we think, in some future human rebirth, conditions will be different and ordinary sensory delight will not be a problem. Perception of nondelight in the whole world requires us to recognize that any rebirth within samsara, no matter how exalted, will be characterized by impermanence and suffering.

Among the ten fetters, those deeply rooted negative habits of mind that meditation works to destroy, are craving for fine material existence and craving for immaterial existence. These realms of existence are primarily mental rather than physical. They are linked to our attainment of the jhana states in meditation. Perception of nondelight in the whole world requires us to abandon hope for rebirth even in one of these exalted mental states.

Instead, the Buddha is saying, we must use the confidence we gain by clear perception of the truth of our situation to cross over doubt and fear and set our sights on nibbana, permanent freedom from the suffering of rebirth. Nothing less will do for Girimananda and for us as well. As the Buddha said in the Mahamangala Sutta:

A mind unshaken
When touched by the worldly states,
Sorrowless, stainless, and secure;
This is the blessing supreme.

· 12 ·

PERCEPTION OF IMPERMANENCE IN REGARD TO ALL MENTAL FORMATIONS

"And what, Ananda, is the perception of impermanence in all conditioned phenomena? Here, a bhikkhu is repelled, humiliated, and disgusted by all conditioned phenomena. This is called the perception of impermanence in all conditioned phenomena." (*tr. Bhikkhu Bodhi*)

WE ARE NOW approaching the last step in our meditative progress toward liberation from suffering. Up to this point, we have used the mind and its internal processes to move along the Buddha's path. We used the mind's powers of concentration to focus our attention on the body and its parts, discovering that the body, like every other conditioned phenomenon, is inconstant, subject to decay and disease, and empty of anything that can be called a "self." Next, we meditated on abandoning the causes of suffering and on adopting instead the mature attitude of dispassion toward the experiences of this life, even the pleasurable experiences of deep meditation. Dispassion helped us to reach the next stage, appreciation of the state beyond the suffering of impermanence—cessation, nibbana. Recognizing that this deathless state is the only worthwhile goal, we meditated on overcoming the wish for rebirth of any kind, even in exalted states of being that are beyond physical suffering.

Now, in this ninth perception, our meditation leads us to give up clinging to all conceptions, all formations, all conditioned and compounded things, including the processes of our own mind. When the Buddha spoke of "all conditioned phenomena," he meant to include all wholesome mental formations, unwholesome mental formations, and imperturbable mental formations. Imperturbable mental formations are those mind states that we develop through the practice of the jhanas. Whatever mental states we gain with the attainment of jhanas are also impermanent.

Sometimes our thoughts seem to be so profound and special that we feel that they should be preserved in some kind of permanent recording system so that they last forever. Unfortunately, even these special thoughts are impermanent. Knowing this, we realize that holding to any thought, however lofty, ends in suffering. This awareness prompts us to let go. Letting go of mental formations frees us from the burden of possessing them.

We are disgusted, even horrified, by the prospect of continuing to cling to anything, even to perception itself. Perception, we realize, is also a compounded phenomenon, made up of the six senses and their objects, plus attention, contact, feeling, and consciousness. With this final step, relinquishing even the perceptual processes that we have used to reach this point, we arrive at the threshold of the unconditioned, nibbana, the state in which all taints of desire have been eliminated and all impermanent, suffering, and selfless formations of any possible rebirth have been discarded. We are ready to complete our journey on the Buddha's path. As the Buddha described this final stage to his monks in the Vatthupama Sutta:

> When he knows and sees thus, his mind is liberated from
> the taint of sensual desire, from the taint of being, and from

the taint of ignorance. When it is liberated, there comes the knowledge: "It is liberated." He understands: "Birth is destroyed, the holy life has been lived, what had to be done has been done, there is no more coming to any state of being." (tr. Bhikkhu Bodhi)

As we can easily see, the Buddha's prescription for healing Girimananda is much more comprehensive than simply eliminating the discomfort of a particular illness. It leads Girimananda and us toward the permanent healing of liberation.

· 13 ·

MINDFULNESS OF BREATHING

"And what, Ananda, is mindfulness of breathing? Here, a bhikkhu, having gone to the forest, to the foot of a tree, or to an empty hut, sits down. Having folded his legs crosswise, straightened his body, and established mindfulness in front of him, just mindful he breathes in, mindful he breathes out.

"Breathing in long, he knows: 'I breathe in long'; or breathing out long, he knows: 'I breathe out long.' Breathing in short, he knows: 'I breathe in short'; or breathing out short, he knows: 'I breathe out short.' He trains thus: 'Experiencing the whole body, I will breathe in'; he trains thus: 'Experiencing the whole body, I will breathe out.' He trains thus: 'Tranquilizing the bodily activity, I will breathe in'; he trains thus: 'Tranquilizing the bodily activity, I will breathe out.'

"He trains thus: 'Experiencing rapture, I will breathe in'; he trains thus: 'Experiencing rapture, I will breathe out.' He trains thus: 'Experiencing happiness, I will breathe in'; he trains thus: 'Experiencing happiness, I will breathe out.' He trains thus: 'Experiencing the mental activity, I will breathe in'; he trains thus: 'Experiencing the mental activity, I will breathe out.' He trains thus: 'Tranquilizing the mental activity, I will breathe in'; he trains thus: 'Tranquilizing the mental activity, I will breathe out.'

"He trains thus: 'Experiencing the mind, I will breathe in'; he trains thus: 'Experiencing the mind, I will breathe out.' He trains thus: 'Gladdening the mind, I will breathe in'; he trains thus: 'Gladdening the mind, I will breathe out.' He trains thus: 'Concentrating the mind, I will breathe in'; he trains thus: 'Concentrating the mind, I will breathe out.' He trains thus:

'Liberating the mind, I will breathe in'; he trains thus: 'Liberating the mind, I will breathe out.'

"He trains thus: 'Contemplating impermanence, I will breathe in'; he trains thus: 'Contemplating impermanence, I will breathe out.' He trains thus: 'Contemplating fading away, I will breathe in'; he trains thus: 'Contemplating fading away, I will breathe out.' He trains thus: 'Contemplating cessation, I will breathe in'; he trains thus: 'Contemplating cessation, I will breathe out.' He trains thus: 'Contemplating relinquishment, I will breathe in'; he trains thus: 'Contemplating relinquishment, I will breathe out.'

"This is called mindfulness of breathing.

"If, Ananda, you visit the bhikkhu Girimananda and speak to him about these ten perceptions, it is possible that on hearing about them he will immediately recover from his affliction."

Then, when the Venerable Ananda had learned these ten perceptions from the Blessed One, he went to the Venerable Girimananda and spoke to him about them. When the Venerable Girimananda heard about these ten perceptions, his affliction immediately subsided. The Venerable Girimananda recovered from that affliction, and that is how he was cured of his affliction. (*tr. Bhikkhu Bodhi*)

....

Pure Perception of the Pure Breath

THE TENTH HEALING PERCEPTION, mindfulness of breathing, is very important. As we gain experience in practicing meditation on the breath, the first thing we notice is that we are able to perceive each part of our inhalation and exhalation without distortion. Nothing can distort the breath. Paying total, undivided attention to this pure breath, our perception becomes increasingly pure. Pure perception of the pure breath calms the mind, relaxes the body, and accelerates our ability to heal from illness. At the same time, we gain proficiency in concentration and mindfulness, both of which are powerful contributors to mental health.

Mindfulness of breathing is also instructive. When we use meditation on the breath to examine the mind-body system as it is, we gain insight into a number of essential dhamma points. As the Buddha explained, "All dhammas arise from attention." We have already noted that we can use mindfulness of breathing to gain firsthand knowledge of the five aggregates—form, feeling, perception, thought, and consciousness. When we perceive the five aggregates of the breath with mindful attention, we notice that each consists of three minor moments: the rising moment, the living moment, and the passing away moment. The same is true of all things that exist. This activity never stops. It is the nature of impermanence. The touch of the breath on the nostrils as we inhale and exhale and the feelings, perceptions, and thoughts that arise in consciousness as we breathe don't stick around. They cease without leaving a trace. Once they are gone, they are gone forever. New forms, feelings, perceptions, thoughts, and consciousness always appear. Observing these changes teaches us detachment and makes it easier for us to relinquish the habit of clinging to any part of the body or mind.

In addition, mindfulness of breathing supports clear and focused meditation on the other nine perceptions. When we reach the tenth perception, we use this clarity and stability to meditate on the four foundations of mindfulness: mindfulness of the body, mindfulness of feelings, mindfulness of mind, and mindfulness of dhamma or phenomena. As a result of these meditations, the seven factors of enlightenment develop within us. These factors—mindfulness, investigation into phenomena, energy, joy, tranquility, concentration, and equanimity—arise in succession, each stage leading to the next. They lead us toward the attainment of "stream entry"—the first stage of enlightenment.

Four Foundations of Mindfulness

The four foundations of mindfulness are presented in the Giri-mananda Sutta as a series of sixteen meditation subjects. Each of the sixteen subjects has two parts: breathing in and breathing out. The sixteen subjects can be divided into four groups. Each group of four, or "tetrad," corresponds to one of the four foundations of mindful-ness. At the most advanced level of meditation, the four meditation subjects in the first tetrad on mindfulness of the body correspond to four cycles of breathing in and breathing out, in other words, eight individual breaths, one after the other! There were monks in the time of the Buddha who attained enlightenment as quickly as that due to their clear comprehension and perfect mindfulness. Here is a break-down of the meditation subjects in each tetrad:

MINDFULNESS OF THE BODY

- ▸ Breathing in long; breathing out long
- ▸ Breathing in short: breathing out short
- ▸ Breathing in experiencing the whole body; breathing out experi-encing the whole body
- ▸ Breathing in tranquilizing the bodily activity: breathing out tranquilizing the bodily activity

MINDFULNESS OF FEELINGS

- ▸ Breathing in experiencing rapture; breathing out experiencing rapture
- ▸ Breathing in experiencing happiness; breathing out experiencing happiness
- ▸ Breathing in experiencing mental activity; breathing out experi-encing mental activity

▶ Breathing in tranquilizing the mental activity: breathing out tranquilizing the mental activity

MINDFULNESS OF MIND

▶ Breathing in experiencing the mind; breathing out experiencing the mind
▶ Breathing in gladdening the mind; breathing out gladdening the mind
▶ Breathing in concentrating the mind; breathing out concentrating the mind
▶ Breathing in liberating the mind; breathing out causing liberating the mind

MINDFULNESS OF PHENOMENA OR DHAMMA

▶ Breathing in contemplating impermanence; breathing out contemplating impermanence
▶ Breathing in contemplating fading away; breathing out contemplating fading away
▶ Breathing in contemplating cessation; breathing out contemplating cessation
▶ Breathing in contemplating relinquishment; breathing out contemplating relinquishment

In the Anapanasati Sutta, the Buddha explains in more detail how to meditate on the four foundations of mindfulness. We begin by meditating on the first tetrad, mindfulness of the body, as follows:

On that occasion a bhikkhu abides contemplating the body as a body, ardent, fully aware, and mindful, having put away covetousness and grief for the world. I say that this is a certain body among the bodies, namely, in-breathing

and out-breathing. That is why on that occasion a bhikkhu abides contemplating the body as a body, ardent, fully
aware, and mindful, having put away covetousness and grief
for the world. (tr. Bhikkhu Bodhi)

The focus of this first meditation is the "breath-body," the form or
body that arises as we breathe in and breathe out. We experience the
breath as a body when its form or shape gives rise to pressure, release,
and other sensations of touch in the nose, lungs, and abdomen. The
breath-body, the sutta continues, is a "body among the bodies." In
other words, it is one of the many bodies, or parts, that make up the
human form. Full awareness and pure mindfulness of even one of the
thirty-two parts of the body can be enough for some meditators to
achieve insight.

Moreover, when we meditate on the breath-body as a "body among
the bodies," we remain focused on the body in and of itself, seeing
the body as simply part of the form aggregate, without the usual colorations of attachment or "covetousness" for the pleasant parts and
"grief" or aversion toward the unpleasant or decaying parts. Like all
forms, the body comes into being, remains present for a time, and then
passes away. Since it is not "myself," there is no reason for us to feel
attached to the body or to grieve when the body gets sick or decays as
a result of aging.

In addition, we recognize that the breath, like all other bodies, is
made up of elements—earth, water, air, and fire. We can recognize the
four elements by their characteristic functions. The function of the
earth element is to generate hardness or softness. The sensations we
experience in the body when we breathe are due to the presence of the
hardness or softness of the breath's earth element. Similarly, we notice
that the breath feels dry when its water element is low. When we are
aware of moisture in the breath, it is because the water element is high.

The function of the air element is motion and energy. We experience the movement of the breath because of its air element. The temperature of the breath is due to its fire element. Heat fluctuates. When the heat element in the breath is high, we call the breath hot. When it drops down, we call the breath cool.

In addition to the four elements, the parts of the body—including the breath—are described as internal or external. The elements inside the body are internal; those outside are external. If we think about this distinction, it may occur to us that the breath that we have inhaled is internal. When we exhale, this internal breath mixes with the external air. Then the breath is external. We might also say that the internal body is inhaling, and the external body is exhaling.

In the Maharahulovada Sutta, the Buddha explained the meaning of the words "internal" and "external" as they apply to the four elements of the body. In terms of the air element, he said, "Whatever internally, belonging to oneself, is air . . . that is up-going winds, down-going winds, winds in limbs, in-breath and out-breath . . . this is called the internal air element." Moreover, the Buddha explained, "Both the internal air element and the external air element are simply air element." This point is important because of our tendency to cling to things we perceive as belonging to us. Seen with "proper wisdom," we recognize that even the air we inhale—the internal air—"is not mine, this I am not, and this is not my self. When one sees it thus as it actually is . . . one becomes disenchanted with the air element and makes the mind dispassionate toward the air element."

Further, the Buddha continues, from time to time, the external air element is disturbed. It "sweeps away villages, towns, cities, districts, and countries," as it does in a hurricane or tornado. At other times, such as during the last month of the hottest part of the year, people "seek wind by means of a fan or bellows, and even the stands of straw in the drip-fringe of the thatch do not stir." These seasonal changes in the external air, which all of us have experienced, demonstrate vividly that the air element, "great as it is, is seen to be impermanent, subject to destruction, disappearance, and change." The same applies to the earth, water, and fire elements inside the body and outside the body. Since this is so, the Buddha asked, "what of this body, which is clung to by craving and lasts but a while?" Our body, too, he reminded us, is composed of four elements, which are always being destroyed, disappearing, or changing. Therefore, he concluded, "There can be no considering that as 'I' or 'mine' or 'I am.'"

We meditate on the second tetrad, mindfulness of feelings, to develop the perception of joy, the perception of happiness, the perception of the mental formations, and the perception of tranquility of mental formations. These perceptions remind us that like the body, feelings can be subdivided. At any given moment, we are able to notice only one kind of feeling—pleasant, unpleasant, or neutral feelings. As with forms, feelings arise, remain present for a time, and pass away.

We train ourselves to regard feelings in this impartial way to undercut the mistaken belief that feelings are solid and reliable, or that pleasant feelings will always remain pleasant. Instead, we develop simple awareness of whatever feeling is arising in the present moment. We recognize that any feeling is just one feeling among many feelings that arise and pass away. In this way, we demonstrate to ourselves that feelings are not "me" and not aspects of "myself." When they are viewed with ardent, fully aware mindfulness, even feelings of intense pain can be experienced without aversion and without desire for conditions to be different. In a similar way, we train ourselves to regard feelings of joy and happiness that arise as a result of our meditation as simply "mental formations" that become "tranquil" when we perceive them with pure mindfulness.

We can also use mindfulness of the breath to explore the nature of the mind. Generally, we are aware of the mind only when we pay attention to the thoughts, concepts, and emotions that arise, remain for a moment, and pass away. But when the mind is composed and steadied by ardent, alert, and mindful concentration, the mind is "released" and moves beyond all concepts, including the concepts of "rejoicing" and grieving.

Finally, we use the breath to meditate on four essential points of the Dhamma: impermanence, dispassion, cessation, and relinquishment or abandonment. Here we focus the mind on mental qualities in and of themselves. Recognizing the impermanence of everything, we experience dispassion. Dispassion means that we see reality as it is and act wisely by not trying to resist it. Dispassion does not mean that we ignore corruption, prejudice, discrimination, or other moral wrongs. We do what we can to correct the problems that we see, but we also understand that our efforts are only a small part of the conditions that bring troubling situations into existence. We also know that there are some aspects of reality that we cannot do anything to change. We grow old. We lose our strength. We die. What can we do about these changes? They are the nature of reality. All we can do is accept them. Dispassion is impartial acceptance of reality as it is. A dispassionate attitude helps us to reach the goal of cessation—the relinquishment or abandoning of all greed and distress and the development of the special mindfulness that is the first of the seven factors of enlightenment.

However, it may not be necessary for us to meditate on all four tetrads. Even just the first tetrad, mindfulness of the body, can be sufficient for a meditator to develop the seven factors of enlightenment. However, if we do not succeed in developing the seven factors by meditating on mindfulness of the body, we try the second tetrad. If we are unable to attain all of the factors by the end of the second, we try the third. If that meditation does not help us reach our goal, we move on to the fourth. This strategy reflects the Buddha's understanding that meditators differ in terms of their capacities and levels of spiritual development. The meditations on mindfulness of the thirty-two solid and liquid parts of the body are quite straightforward and thus effective for most meditators. However, the Buddha made clear that all seven factors of enlightenment can arise as a result of mindfulness meditation on any one of the four tetrads.

The Seven Factors of Enlightenment

We meditate on the four foundations of mindfulness in order to develop the seven factors of enlightenment. In the Anapanasati Sutta, the Buddha explained how each of the seven factors arises in succession, each stage leading to the next.

We attain the first factor, *mindfulness*, when we experience unremitting mindfulness on any meditation subject, such as a part of the body. In order for our mindfulness to become a factor of enlightenment, it must be ardent, fully aware, and free of attachment and aversion. When such mindfulness is aroused, it must be developed by unremitting practice, through which mindfulness "comes to fulfillment" as a factor of enlightenment.

When unremitting mindfulness has been established, the meditator examines that state with wisdom and embarks upon a full inquiry into it. The practice begins with careful attention to discriminating between right and wrong, wholesome and unwholesome, blameable and blameless, inferior and superior, dark and bright states of mind and being. However, it is not necessary for the meditator to discriminate between internal and external states—those that arise within the body and mind and those that are external to the body and mind.

For instance, a meditator might choose to investigate the eye consciousness and visual objects such as flowers. As we have said, when an external flower meets the eye, eye consciousness arises internally. When the eye, the flower, and consciousness meet, contact arises. Then feeling and perception arise in the mind. Even as they are arising, the flower, the eye, and consciousness itself are changing and passing away. Recognizing this impermanence, the meditator's pleasure in enjoying the beauty, fragrance, and freshness of the flower vanishes. From this investigation, the meditator concludes that the internal eye and eye consciousness and all external visual objects such as flowers and mountains are impermanent, suffering, and selfless. As the meditator's perception of this truth deepens and becomes universal, the factor of *investigation of phenomena* develops, eventually coming to fulfillment as a factor of enlightenment.

Now the meditator continues these investigations with tireless energy, and by doing so, arouses the *energy* factor of enlightenment, which practice deepens and brings to fulfillment. This energy causes the fourth factor, *joy* or rapture, to arise in the meditator, which by repeated practice comes to fulfillment as a factor of enlightenment. Joy makes the body and mind tranquil and arouses, develops, and brings to fulfillment the *tranquility* factor of enlightenment. When the meditator's body and mind are tranquil, the feeling of pleasure arouses the meditator's concentration, which develops and comes to fulfillment as the *concentration* factor of enlightenment. Finally, the meditator looks closely and with equanimity at the mind thus concentrated, which arouses, develops, and brings to fulfillment the *equanimity* factor of enlightenment.

The Buddha also explained that the meditator must discriminate between suitable and less suitable occasions for cultivating the various factors of enlightenment. For instance, when the mind is sluggish, it is not a good time to develop the enlightenment factors of tranquility, concentration, or equanimity. The Buddha used a simple analogy in the Bojjangasamyutta to explain his reasoning:

> Just as when a man wants to make a small fire flare up, if he throws wet grass, green leaves and wet sticks into it, sprays it with water, and scatters soil over it, he would not be able to make that small fire flare up. (tr. Bhikkhu Bodhi)

Rather, when the mind is sluggish, the meditator should cultivate the enlightenment factors of investigation, energy, and rapture, which arouse and uplift the mind.

In a similar way, when the mind is overly excited, it is not a suitable time to meditate on cultivating the enlightenment factors of investigation of phenomena, energy, or rapture:

> Just as when a man wants to extinguish a great bonfire, if he does not throw dry grass, dry leaves, and dry sticks into it, or blow on it, and does not scatter soil over it, he would not be able to extinguish that great bonfire. (tr. Bhikkhu Bodhi)

Rather, when the mind is excited, the meditator should cultivate calming factors, such as tranquility, concentration, and equanimity. Doing so, the Buddha explained, is like throwing wet grass, green leaves, and wet sticks into a great bonfire, spraying it with water, and scattering soil over it.

In other words, building on the foundation of the ten perceptions, we can cultivate the seven factors or qualities we need to achieve enlightenment. But we must be careful and mindful, applying our discriminating wisdom to determine when and how to cultivate each of the factors while keeping the mind balanced—rousing it when it is sluggish and calming it down when it is overly excited. Though the process might seem complex and the goal of total freedom from suffering lofty and hard to reach, the tenth perception reminds us that the entire path to liberation begins with simple mindfulness of breathing in and breathing out!

PART 3: MEDITATION
ON PERCEPTION

· 14 ·

MEDITATION: IMPERMANENCE
AND SIX SENSORY OBJECTS

NOW THAT we have some understanding of the ten healing perceptions, let's look more closely at the first of these—the perception of impermanence. In the meditations that follow, we use mindfulness of breathing as the basis for vipassana or insight meditation aimed at attaining direct perception of impermanence. Anyone can see impermanence superficially. But doing so is not enough to make a difference in our lives. We need to see impermanence deeply in our own experiences. In our meditation, we pay total mindful attention to the processes of our own body and mind without assumptions or preconceived notions. This impartial attention allows the mind to see impermanence from its roots. Direct, preconceptual knowledge of impermanence opens the door to seeing the truth about all conditioned things.

Insight meditation, as we said, is meditation that uses mindfulness to investigate phenomena. When we practice insight meditation, we can use any object as the point of focus, since all objects have the same universal characteristics. Whether we focus on the breath, on one of the parts of the body, or on feelings, perceptions, thoughts, or consciousness, we discover the same three truths: the impermanence, suffering, and selflessness of all forms, feelings, perceptions, thoughts, consciousness, sights, sounds, smells, tastes, touches, and mind objects. While breathing in and out, these are the things that we experience.

The entire practice of Buddhist meditation begins with seeing the truth of impermanence. The very moment Siddhartha Gotama, the Buddha-to-be, saw impermanence in the deepest way, his mind opened to the rest of his discovery—dispassion, cessation, and abandonment. With perfect mindfulness, the Buddha saw impermanence in forms, feelings, perceptions, thoughts, and consciousness arising and passing away along with the breath. He used this basic truth to deepen his insight, liberate his mind from attachment to impermanent things, and overcome the fetters that bound him to the cycle of suffering. By diligent practice of meditations such as the ones below, we can do the same.

We begin by using mindfulness to become aware of the process of perception. As we recall, perception takes place in the mind as a result of the contact between a sensory object, one of the body's six senses, and consciousness. When we pay attention to this process with careful mindfulness, we become aware that every aspect of our perception is always changing—the sensory objects themselves change, our attention to these objects changes, and our consciousness changes as we perceive them. In the end, all we perceive are changes.

▶ We begin each meditation by practicing mindfulness of breathing as described on pages 87 to 99.

▶ Once the body is relaxed and the mind is peaceful, we turn our attention to the perceptions of the six kinds of sensory objects: sights, sounds, smells, tastes, touches, and mental objects.

▶ For instance, we listen to the sounds of birds—pigeons, sparrows, nightingales, blue jays, parrots, or other birds. We notice that some make loud and annoying sounds, and others make sweet and attractive sounds. We listen as well to sounds made by humans. Just like the birds, some make loud and annoying sounds. Others make soft and agreeable sounds. As we listen, we notice that whatever sound we hear is always changing. When we listen to sounds mindfully—without anger, greed, or delusion—all we hear is change and impermanence.

► Next, we may turn our attention to the sense of smell. We breathe in the scent of fresh flowers or the smell of soap, cow dung, or bread baking and pay total mindful attention. Whatever smell we notice is changing all the time.

► Next, we pay attention to the touch of our clothes against the skin—loose or tight, soft or rough, soothing or scratchy, changing all the time. We experience the touch of the cushion we are sitting on, and how this perception changes from soft and comfortable to hard and unyielding. We experience these changing sensations with awareness.

► If we open our eyes, we see leaves, trees, and clouds that are moving. Everything the eyes can see is moving and changing in obvious and subtle ways.

► Now we notice that everything we perceive is changing. There is no particular order for things to arise. While being aware of a sound, we suddenly become aware of the impermanence of a feeling, or a thought, or of consciousness itself. We allow the mind to experience these changes in whatever order they arise. No matter what object the mind becomes aware of, we notice impermanence in that object. We don't have to force ourselves to see it. Impermanence is right there, very clearly marked. Everything we perceive is clearly marked with impermanence.

► Similarly, all kinds of feelings—pleasant, unpleasant, or neutral—that arise from the eyes, ears, nose, tongue, and body are changing all the time.

► When thoughts arise—wholesome, unwholesome, or neutral—

we pay total mindful attention to them. All we notice in them is change.

► Any perception that arises depending on sight, sound, smell, taste, touch, or thought always changes. Any state of consciousness that arises depending on sight, sound, smell, taste, touch, and thought also changes. While we are paying attention to any of them, it changes.

► Underneath all changes is the breath, and it is also changing. The feeling of the breath, the perception of breath, the attention to breath, the intention to pay attention to breath, and the awareness of breath—they are all changing, without any power that can stop the change. Nothing can prevent the change of anything.

► When we breathe in, even the breath does not remain static. It changes by itself. It goes to our lungs, exchanges oxygen with carbon dioxide, and then leaves the lungs. We don't do anything to cause this changing process. It happens by itself.

► Our heartbeat, the blood circulating through the capillaries and arteries—these movements take place naturally through the very same process of impermanence. Radiating body heat and absorbing environmental heat to balance the body's temperature take place due to impermanence. Heat in the body must move, air in the body must move, liquid in the body must move, other elements in the body must move naturally in order to keep the body going. All bodily functions take place naturally due to impermanence. We use mindfulness to become aware of this process while breathing. If we cannot be fully aware of all of these simultaneous changes, we strive to be aware of whatever we can notice while breathing in and out.

► Then we realize that change is the nature of all the forms, feelings, perceptions, thoughts, and consciousness of everyone and everything in the universe. They all change constantly. With this understanding we breathe. We feel that we are breathing with the rest of the world, which experiences the changes the same way that we do.

▸ Although we may wish to stop change in its tracks and grip the present moment tightly, doing so is impossible. The processes of life don't stop, not for a split second. Our attempt to freeze the present moment in place is like trying to catch air in our fist. Instead, the mindful mind lets it all happen without longing for things to be different or bemoaning our fate. This attitude is known as abandonment. While noticing impermanence, nonfixity, cessation, and abandonment, we breathe in and breathe out.

▸ Noticing these changes without greed, hatred, and delusion is our practice of mindfulness. We realize that the breath, feeling, perception, attention, intention, all kinds of thoughts, and consciousness are there to help us to gain insight into the reality of impermanence. Anyone paying total undivided attention to the breath, feeling, perception, thought, attention, intention, and consciousness can experience the same changes that we experience.

· 15 ·

MEDITATION: THE MIND
IS ALSO CHANGING

As we watch the changing nature of our experiences, we notice
that the mind does not remain static when it becomes aware
of the changes in conditioned things. We discover that the mind also
changes when it notices changes in other things. The mind is not an
immovable mover. The very notion of an immovable mover is illogical.
A nonmover cannot notice the movement of another object without
moving itself. While the object is moving, the subject must also move
to notice the movement of the object.

In other words, our awareness of impermanence is also impermanent. That is why the mind, while watching the impermanence of
feelings, drifts away from this awareness. While being mindful of the
changes of one sound, we hear another sound. Then, leaving the first
sound, the mind goes to the second sound. This shift of focus shows us
that the mind watching the impermanence of one thing is also changing. It moves itself in order to notice the changes in its objects.

While we are watching the changes in one perception, another
perception arises. Then the mind goes there and notices its change.
While being engaged in it, another perception arises. Then the mind
goes there. So, as the perception arises, reaches its peak, and passes
away, the mind follows these steps. Sometimes, before one perception
moves from one step to the next, the mind moves to another object.
The mind does not stay still observing one object to see the completion

of the three steps of change—the rising moment, peak moment, and passing away moment. Observing and noticing are dynamic functions or activities.

We may notice the changes in our feelings—pleasant, unpleasant, or neutral. While we are engaged in noticing the changes of feeling, suddenly we hear a sound. Then, the mind goes there, interrupting the awareness of the change that is taking place in our feelings. But we should not be disappointed. Rather, we are simply aware of the fact that the mind that has been noticing the changes in our feelings is also changing.

Even our knowledge of dhamma is subject to impermanence. Things change, so truth can become lie, as the Dvayatanupassana Sutta tells us:

> Look at the world including gods
> That thinks nonself as self.
> Having entered into the mentality and materiality,
> They think, "This is true."
> Whatever way they think,
> It changes into another thing.
> Making it untrue.
> This is the nature of impermanent things.
> Having realized that
> Nibbāna is unchanging truth,
> The Noble Ones attain it
> Leaving no trace behind.

The message here is that every time we believe that something is permanent, pleasant, a source of happiness, and a lasting self, it changes and becomes its opposite. This is the nature of impermanence. When we see this truth deeply, we finally stop chasing phantoms. Getting to this point requires mindfulness and concentration. When mindfulness and concentration are stable and work together as a team, we notice countless subtle changes taking place simultaneously in our mind and body. Deep mindfulness becomes aware of the slightest change and sheds light on this change. Strong concentration coupled with mindfulness focuses the mind so that we can see the workings of impermanence clearly.

▸ To experience the mind's changes experientially, follow the steps given above for meditating on the impermanence of the six sensory objects. This time, focus not on the changes in the objects of perception, but on the changes in the mind that is perceiving these objects.

▸ Notice clearly how often the mind alters its perceptual focus, switching instantaneously from external to internal objects. Notice that the mind, along with everything else that exists, is engaged in constant and unstoppable change.

· 16 ·

MEDITATION: THE KEYS TO OUR DELIVERANCE

THERE ARE THREE THINGS that we need to know directly, absolutely, down to the marrow of our bones. They are impermanence, suffering, and selflessness. They are the keys to our deliverance. Impermanence is the entry point, the building block, on which the other two depend. If we see impermanence deeply, suffering and selflessness are the direct, inescapable conclusions.

- ► When we practice mindfulness meditation, we see things changing. We see impermanence deeply, down to the most incredibly fast, instant-to-instant level.
- ► Then we see it more broadly. We perceive impermanence in everything we see and everything we could ever see.
- ► When we are deeply conscious of impermanence in all of our experiences, the mind gets tired of the incessant change. This is the suffering we experience in impermanence. Buddha discovered this truth and explained it to us by saying, "Whatever is impermanent is suffering."

"Whatever is impermanent is suffering" is a figure of speech, like the phrase "a sleeping village." It is not the village that sleeps but the beings that live there—humans and animals—that are sleeping. In the same way, it is not the impermanent things themselves that are suffering. If everything impermanent suffered, then trees, tables, rocks, and other objects should suffer, since they are impermanent. Also, if it is impermanence that makes a being suffer, then even the Buddhas and those beings who have attained enlightenment would suffer, since these beings do experience impermanence. The reason these beings do not suffer is that they are not attached to impermanent things. The same applies to us. As long as we are attached to impermanent things, we experience suffering. To end our suffering, we must end our attachment to things that are constantly changing.

▸ Among these impermanent things are the aggregates of our own body and mind. When we perceive the suffering in all of the aggregates of our experience, we become disenchanted with the aggregates.

▸ Being disenchanted helps us to become dispassionate. Passion, we realize, is the glue that holds the "self" and the world together. When this gluing power is removed, abandonment arises, which leads to the cessation of our suffering.

▸ To reach this goal, it is important that our mindfulness and attention are pure, which means that they are without concepts. At this level of meditation, ideas and thoughts are like thorns, boils, wounds, or impediments. When concepts are absent, we can focus the mind like a laser beam on the five aggregates.

▸ With the clarity of this laser-like perspective, the mind can see that "I" exists only when the body, feelings, perceptions, thoughts, and consciousness exist. They, in turn, exist within the parameters of impermanence. Impermanence burns everything. We don't find any "self" or "soul" or "I" in any of the aggregates.

▸ Suppose we put many components together and made a flute. When we blow it, it makes a sweet sound. Suppose someone breaks this flute into little pieces in search of the sound in the flute. That person will never find the sound! In the same way, we will never find the "I" in the aggregates, no matter how finely we break them down. That is our discovery of selflessness.

▸ Not seeing impermanence, we cling to impermanent things. The more we cling, the more we suffer, because impermanent things betray us when we try to hold on to them. They deceive us into believing that some thing or person can give us permanent happiness. Circumstances cheat us. Relationships grow difficult. People die. Jobs change. Seeing the impermanence of everything, we take precautions against their deceptive, constantly arising and departing nature. This is our discovery of the suffering nature of all conditioned things.

▸ As we progress in our mindfulness, we increasingly recognize that impermanence, suffering, and selflessness are qualities not only of the aggregates of our own body and mind, but also of everything that arises depending on causes and conditions.

▸ Seeing this truth, we are disappointed with the aggregates and, in fact, with every conditioned thing. We recognize that pleasure and pain are actually two sides of the same coin. When we experience pleasure, we wish to hold on to that pleasurable feeling. When we experience pain, we wish to get rid of that unpleasant feeling and experience a pleasant feeling. Both are wishes. Both are craving. When we see that suffering is inherent in pleasure, we become disappointed with pleasure. That is dispassion.

· 17 ·

MEDITATION:
DEPENDENT ORIGINATION

WHEN THIS IS, that is. When this arises, that arises. When this ceases, that ceases." These important words introduce the Buddha's teaching of dependent origination. They tell us that everything arises dependent on causes and conditions and passes away dependent on causes and conditions. To clarify this point, the Buddha said: "Decay and death, bhikkhus, are impermanent, conditionally come into existence, dependently arise, fading, of the nature of fading away, of the nature of passing away, and of the nature of cessation."

Many people who listened to the Dhamma, such as Venerable Kondanna—one of the original five disciples of the Buddha—attained the first stage of enlightenment by contemplating the impermanence of all conditioned things. The Venerable Kondanna expressed his realization of impermanence in words that are now well known: "That which is of the nature of arising is also of the nature of passing."

Not seeing the dependent nature of everything, ordinary people fall into extreme views. One extreme is that everything exists permanently, and the other is that nothing exists. But when people see with wisdom that everything that exists arises depending on causes and conditions, the notion that nothing exists vanishes. Similarly, when they see with wisdom that everything that passes away does so depending on causes and conditions, the notion that everything exists permanently vanishes as well.

Rising and falling is the nature of impermanence. In insight meditation, this understanding is known as the wisdom of rising and passing away. From the beginning of insight meditation, we focus our attention on the rising and falling of the breath, feelings, perception, thoughts, and consciousness. Also, we focus attention on the rising and falling of contact and attention, two factors of the mind that arise along with the senses when they meet their respective objects. Seeing rising and falling, wise individuals accelerate their practice by arousing spiritual urgency. Those persons who have seen impermanence as it really is are not shaken by worldly vicissitudes.

▶ We don't need to do anything to make anything impermanent. Impermanence is there all the time. All we do is become aware of impermanence.

▶ We don't need to do anything to create nonattachment. Because of impermanence, nonattachment to impermanent things arises by itself.

▶ We don't need to do anything to cause anything to cease. Cessation takes place by itself.

▶ Similarly we don't need to do anything to abandon anything. When things cease, abandoning is right there.

▶ Every movement in the body takes place without stopping. Nothing sticks together. The various parts of the physical body cooperate but do not cling to each other. Each part supports the others in their natural and essential changes. This is an example for us of nonattachment.

▶ In any series of activities, every moment must cease in order for the next moment to arise. If the one moment does not cease, the next moment could not arise in the same series of activities. Whether these moments are related to air, fire, water, heat, or earth, one moment arises and ceases in order for the next moment to arise. This is cessation.

▸ Once a moment has ceased, it is gone forever. It cannot be revived by any means. What arises is a new moment. The mindful meditator lets this process happen without trying to resist this change. This is abandonment.

· 18 ·

MEDITATION: SEEING
IMPERMANENCE WITH INSIGHT
AWARENESS

IMPERMANENCE IS THE most slippery truth we have ever encountered! It goes against everything we think or know about existence. The mind resists impermanence subtly. It slides into the mind easily and slides right out again just as easily, without making any impact. And to increase our spiritual development, the perception of impermanence must have impact. Direct experience of impermanence is the basic truth we need to make ourselves free.

Why, we may be wondering, is direct experience of impermanence so important? The simple answer is that when the mind is established in full awareness of impermanence, it naturally loses interest in clinging to anything. What, after all, is there to cling to? Anything we wish to cling to is changing so quickly that there is nothing to grasp. Impermanence dominates everything. Everything disappears without giving us prior notice.

We become mindful of our nonclinging attitude and then naturally allow this mind state to cease by itself, in its own time. Seeing the impermanence of everything awakens the mind to the reality that there is nothing that can stop change. No power, no authority anywhere in the universe can put an end to impermanence. This awareness helps us to realize that there is no "self" pulling the strings, no immovable mover in anything.

We always hear that anything that is impermanent is unsatisfactory. Only when we are experiencing pain are we grateful that something is impermanent. When we experience happiness or, more precisely, excitement, we long for it to remain as a permanent state. Yet regardless of our wishes, things change in their own way and at their own speed.

When we look deeply into our own life experiences, we remember many times when suffering arose because of our attachment to impermanent forms, feelings, perceptions, thoughts, and consciousness. If we truly wish to end our suffering, we must eliminate this attachment. To see impermanence with insight awareness, we must pay total, mindful attention to our experiences without concepts or preconceived notions. This impartial attention opens the mind to recognizing the connection between impermanence and suffering at the root level.

- We begin every day with meditation, using the breath as the primary point of focus. As the breath becomes calm, subtle, and relaxed, the mind becomes calm and relaxed.
- Our meditation is pleasurable. Each moment is a new moment. Each moment is a fresh moment. Each moment brings us new insights and new understanding. We begin to see things that we have never seen before. We attain what we have never attained before. We see things from a totally new perspective. Each new experience brings us refreshment, calm, coolness, joy, and happiness.
- Eventually, we may feel a calm and cool sensation spreading through the entire face, under the eyes, eyebrows, forehead, the middle of the head, and the back of the head. We don't do anything artificial or deliberate to gain this happiness. It happens naturally when the conditions are ripe.
- Then we may experience a very subtle, very peaceful, but very

sharp and clear vibration in our neck, shoulders, and chest area. As we go on breathing normally, simultaneous with this vibration we may experience the expanding and contracting of the entire upper part of the body between the shoulders and the lower part of navel. We may experience each cell throughout the body vibrating and changing, rising and falling with an inconceivable rapidity.

► These sensations do not always arise in the same way and in the same order. Some people experience similar sensations elsewhere in the body or in another progression. It's important that we do not anticipate a particular experience or think that something is wrong if we do not feel it. The point is not the sequence of sensations. The point is what the experience means.

► The sensations remind us that nothing is static. Everything is dynamic. Everything is changing. Everything is appearing and disappearing. Feelings arise. Everything that we think is permanent is in fact impermanent and changing constantly. We cannot make anything stay the same for even two consecutive moments. One moment's experience seems to be pleasant, and the mind wishes to keep it that way. But before the mind even makes this wish, the sensation has changed. The mind moves with inconceivable rapidity. No matter how fast the mind moves to grasp the pleasant experience, the experience changes before the mind reaches it. Its arising is like a dream. Millions of tiny little experiences arise and pass away in an instant. They are like lightening. No, much faster than that. We cannot keep up with the speed of their change.

► We may think, "Let me see the beginning, duration, and passing away of this experience." But before this thought arises, the objects of our sense experience have arisen, reached their maturity, and passed away. Sometimes the mind can catch the beginning of an experience but not the middle or the maturity of it. Or sometimes we may experience the middle of a sensation but not the end of it; or we may catch the end of it but not the middle or the beginning. Nevertheless, we are mindful of the changes. That is good. At least we can notice the changes taking place. It is even better to notice how fast things change. We experience impermanence all day long, all night long, every waking moment.

▸ At this point, we may feel as if we are breathing with the rest of the world. We feel every creature from tiny ants to great elephants, minnows to giant whales, crawling worms to huge pythons. All of them are breathing to our rhythm or we are breathing to theirs.

▸ When we pay total mindful attention to the body, feelings, perceptions, thoughts, and consciousness, we experience every tiny part of them constantly changing. When our mindfulness is established, the mind notices that every split second is new. Every molecule of the body, every feeling, perception, thought, and consciousness itself—they are all changing at unimaginable speed.

▸ The breath moves in and out with this change. The sensations keep changing. Our experience of this change is changing, too. Our attention and the intention to pay attention to noticing the change are changing. Our awareness is changing.

· 19 ·

FREEDOM

THE DHAMMAPADA TELLS US:

> When one sees with wisdom that all conditioned things
> are impermanent, unsatisfactory, and that all the dhammas
> are without self, then one would be disappointed with suf-
> fering, which is the nature of all conditions, conditionings,
> and conditioned things. This is the path to deliverance.

We may be wondering what it means to be disappointed with
suffering. It seems that we must enjoy something first in order to be
disappointed with it. But who, we wonder, enjoys suffering? In truth,
the Buddha explained, any person who enjoys sensual pleasure enjoys
suffering. Since everything is always changing, whatever we find pleasurable eventually changes to suffering. Eating a slice of chocolate cake
might bring us pleasure, but eating the whole cake will almost certainly
change that pleasure to suffering. When we look at the whole picture,
in which we find both pleasure and pain, we gain the understanding
that both suffering and enjoyment come together in one package.
When we recognize that pain is inherent in any kind of pleasure, we
become disappointed with pleasure.

When what we are enjoying disappoints us, we are willing to give
it up and look for something that will not disappoint us. Our attachment to sensual pleasure binds us to this life and to future lives of

similar pleasures and pains. It blocks our attainment of the jhana states of concentration. As our meditation progresses, we see that there is only disappointment in everything that arises in samsara, the realm of conditioned existence. We realize that we are binding ourselves to further revolutions on this endless cycle and develop the desire to free ourselves from it. When we realize the nature of conditioned things, which are marked by impermanence, suffering, and selflessness, we are disappointed with suffering and seek nibbana, unconditioned, permanent, and without self.

This realization motivates us to redouble our meditative efforts to achieve high states of concentration and insight. As we progress through the stages of concentration called the jhanas, eventually we reach a state in which perception itself ceases. In the Concentration Sutta, the Buddha describes this state as one in which the meditator no longer perceives the five elements of which all conditioned things are comprised:

> "It is in this way, Ananda, that a bhikkhu could obtain such a state of concentration that he would not be percipient of earth in relation to earth; of water in relation to water; of fire in relation to fire; of air in relation to air; of the base of the infinity of space in relation to the base of the infinity of space." (tr. Bhikkhu Bodhi)

Nor is the meditator aware of the jhana states through which he/she is passing or indeed of anything in this world or out of it:

> "He would not be percipient of the base of the infinity of consciousness in relation to the base of the infinity of consciousness; of the base of nothingness in relation to the base

of nothingness; of the base of neither-perception-nor-non-perception in relation to the base of neither-percep-tion-nor-nonperception; of this world in relation to this world; of the other world in relation to the other world."
(tr. Bhikkhu Bodhi)

"But," the Buddha explained further, the meditator in this state "would still be percipient." In what way, Ananda asked, is such a meditator perceptive? To which, the Buddha replied:

"Here, Ananda, a bhikkhu is percipient thus: 'This is peaceful, this is sublime, that is, the stilling of all activities, the relinquishing of all acquisitions, the destruction of craving, dispassion, cessation, nibbāna.'" (tr. Bhikkhu Bodhi)

While we are in life, the peaceful and exalted state beyond ordinary perception described here by the Buddha is temporary. It arises from meditative concentration and lasts at most seven days. Yet achieving it is an important step on the path because it foreshadows the final cessation of perception that accompanies the death of a fully enlightened person—nibbana, the cessation of existence, extinction, the state utterly and permanently beyond death and rebirth, the ultimate goal of the Buddha's path.

In the Characteristic of Nonself Sutta given by the Buddha to his first five disciples in the Deer Park near Varanasi soon after he attained enlightenment, thus also known as the Five Brethren Sutta, the Buddha laid out how the path to this exalted place unfolds from the perception that the five aggregates are impermanent, suffering, and selfless:

"Seeing thus, bhikkhus, the instructed noble disciple experiences revulsion toward form, revulsion toward feeling, revulsion toward perception, revulsion toward volitional formations, revulsion toward consciousness. Experiencing revulsion, he becomes dispassionate. Through dispassion [his mind] is liberated. When it is liberated there comes the knowledge: 'It's liberated.' He understands: 'Destroyed is birth, the holy life has been lived, what had to be done has been done, there is no more for this state of being.'" (tr. Bhikkhu Bodhi)

This is the Buddha's path to freedom. It begins with the simple process of examining with mindfulness the ways we ordinarily perceive our own body and mind as well as the world around us. Perception itself is the key. So let's begin. Right now.

APPENDIX
GIRIMĀNANDA SUTTA (AN 10:60)

ON ONE OCCASION the Blessed One was dwelling at Sāvatthī in Jeta's Grove, Anāthapiṇḍika's Park. Now on that occasion the Venerable Girimānanda was sick, afflicted, and gravely ill.

Then the Venerable Ānanda approached the Blessed One, paid homage to him, sat down to one side, and said to him:

"Bhante, the Venerable Girimānanda is sick, afflicted, and gravely ill. It would be good if the Blessed One would visit him out of compassion."

"If, Ānanda, you visit the bhikkhu Girimānanda and speak to him about ten perceptions, it is possible that on hearing about them his affliction will immediately subside. What are the ten?

"(1) The perception of impermanence, (2) the perception of non-self, (3) the perception of unattractiveness, (4) the perception of danger, (5) the perception of abandoning, (6) the perception of dispassion, (7) the perception of cessation, (8) the perception of non-delight in the entire world, (9) the perception of impermanence in all conditioned phenomena, and (10) mindfulness of breathing.

(1) "And what, Ānanda, is the perception of impermanence? Here, having gone to the forest, to the foot of a tree, or to an empty hut, a bhikkhu reflects thus: 'Form is impermanent, feeling is impermanent, perception is impermanent, volitional activities are impermanent, consciousness is impermanent.' Thus he dwells contemplating impermanence in these five aggregates subject to clinging. This is called the perception of impermanence.

(2) "And what, Ānanda, is the perception of non-self? Here, having gone to the forest, to the foot of a tree, or to an empty hut, a bhikkhu reflects thus: 'The eye is non-self, forms are non-self; the ear is non-self, sounds are non-self; the nose is non-self, odors are non-self; the tongue is non-self, tastes are non-self; the body is non-self, tactile objects are non-self; the mind is non-self, mental phenomena are non-self.' Thus he dwells contemplating non-self in these six internal and external sense bases. This is called the perception of non-self.

(3) "And what, Ānanda, is the perception of unattractiveness? Here, a bhikkhu reviews this very body upward from the soles of the feet and downward from the tips of the hairs, enclosed in skin, as full of many kinds of impurities: 'There are in this body hair of the head, hair of the body, nails, teeth, skin, flesh, sinews, bones, bone marrow, kidneys, heart, liver, pleura, spleen, lungs, intestines, mesentery, stomach, excrement, bile, phlegm, pus, blood, sweat, fat, tears, grease, saliva, snot, fluid of the joints, urine.' Thus he dwells contemplating unattractiveness in this body. This is called the perception of unattractiveness.

(4) "And what, Ānanda, is the perception of danger? Here, having gone to the forest, to the foot of a tree, or to an empty hut, a bhikkhu reflects thus: 'This body is the source of much pain and danger; for all sorts of afflictions arise in this body, that is, eye-disease, disease of the inner ear, nose-disease, tongue-disease, body-disease, head-disease, disease of the external ear, mouth-disease, tooth-disease, cough, asthma, catarrh, pyrexia, fever, stomach ache, fainting, dysentery, gripes, cholera, leprosy, boils, eczema, tuberculosis, epilepsy, ringworm, itch, scab, chickenpox, scabies, hemorrhage, diabetes, hemorrhoids, cancer, fistula; illnesses originating from bile, phlegm, wind, or their combination; illnesses produced by change of climate; illnesses produced by careless behavior; illnesses produced by assault; or illnesses produced

as the result of kamma; and cold, heat, hunger, thirst, defecation, and urination.' Thus he dwells contemplating danger in this body. This is called the perception of danger.

(5) "And what, Ānanda, is the perception of abandoning? Here, a bhikkhu does not tolerate an arisen sensual thought; he abandons it, dispels it, terminates it, and obliterates it. He does not tolerate an arisen thought of ill will . . . an arisen thought of harming . . . bad unwholesome states whenever they arise; he abandons them, dispels them, terminates them, and obliterates them. This is called the perception of abandoning.

(6) "And what, Ānanda, is the perception of dispassion? Here, having gone to the forest, to the root of a tree, or to an empty hut, a bhikkhu reflects thus: 'This is peaceful, this is sublime, that is, the stilling of all activities, the relinquishment of all acquisitions, the destruction of craving, dispassion, nibbāna.' This is called the perception of dispassion.

(7) "And what, Ānanda, is the perception of cessation? Here, having gone to the forest, to the root of a tree, or to an empty hut, a bhikkhu reflects thus: 'This is peaceful, this is sublime, that is, the stilling of all activities, the relinquishment of all acquisitions, the destruction of craving, cessation, nibbāna.' This is called the perception of cessation.

(8) "And what, Ānanda, is the perception of non-delight in the entire world? Here, a bhikkhu refrains from any engagement and clinging, mental standpoints, adherences, and underlying tendencies in regard to the world, abandoning them without clinging to them. This is called the perception of non-delight in the entire world.

(9) "And what, Ānanda, is the perception of impermanence in all conditioned phenomena? Here, a bhikkhu is repelled, humiliated, and disgusted by all conditioned phenomena. This is called the perception of impermanence in all conditioned phenomena.

(10) "And what, Ānanda, is mindfulness of breathing? Here, a bhik-khu, having gone to the forest, to the foot of a tree, or to an empty hut, sits down. Having folded his legs crosswise, straightened his body, and established mindfulness in front of him, just mindful he breathes in, mindful he breathes out.

"Breathing in long, he knows: 'I breathe in long'; or breathing out long, he knows: 'I breathe out long.' Breathing in short, he knows: 'I breathe in short'; or breathing out short, he knows: 'I breathe out short.' He trains thus: 'Experiencing the whole body, I will breathe in'; he trains thus: 'Experiencing the whole body, I will breathe out.' He trains thus: 'Tranquilizing the bodily activity, I will breathe in'; he trains thus: 'Tranquilizing the bodily activity, I will breathe out.'

"He trains thus: 'Experiencing rapture, I will breathe in'; he trains thus: 'Experiencing rapture, I will breathe out.' He trains thus: 'Experiencing happiness, I will breathe in'; he trains thus: 'Experiencing happiness, I will breathe out.' He trains thus: 'Experiencing the mental activity, I will breathe in'; he trains thus: 'Experiencing the mental activity, I will breathe out.' He trains thus: 'Tranquilizing the mental activity, I will breathe in'; he trains thus: 'Tranquilizing the mental activity, I will breathe out.'

"He trains thus: 'Experiencing the mind, I will breathe in'; he trains thus: 'Experiencing the mind, I will breathe out.' He trains thus: 'Gladdening the mind, I will breathe in'; he trains thus: 'Gladdening the mind, I will breathe out.' He trains thus: 'Concentrating the mind, I will breathe in'; he trains thus: 'Concentrating the mind, I will breathe out.' He trains thus: 'Liberating the mind, I will breathe in'; he trains thus: 'Liberating the mind, I will breathe out.'

"He trains thus: 'Contemplating impermanence, I will breathe in'; he trains thus: 'Contemplating impermanence, I will breathe out.' He trains thus: 'Contemplating fading away, I will breathe in'; he trains thus: 'Contemplating fading away, I will breathe out.' He trains thus: 'Contemplating cessation, I will breathe in'; he trains thus: 'Contemplating cessation, I will breathe out.' He trains thus: 'Contemplating relinquishment, I will breathe in'; he trains thus: 'Contemplating relinquishment, I will breathe out.'

"This is called mindfulness of breathing.

"If, Ānanda, you visit the bhikkhu Girimānanda and speak to him about these ten perceptions, it is possible that on hearing about them he will immediately recover from his affliction."

Then, when the Venerable Ānanda had learned these ten perceptions from the Blessed One, he went to the Venerable Girimānanda and spoke to him about them. When the Venerable Girimānanda heard about these ten perceptions, his affliction immediately subsided. The Venerable Girimānanda recovered from that affliction, and that is how he was cured of his affliction.

Translated from the Pāli by Bhikkhu Bodhi in *The Numerical Discourses of the Buddha: A Translation of the Aṅguttara Nikāya* (Boston: Wisdom Publications, 2012), 1411–15.

GLOSSARY

abandonment: Watching the mind to identify and get rid of unskillful or unwholesome thoughts, ideas, and impulses before they ripen into negative actions.

aggregates: The five traditional constituents of body and mind: form, feeling, perception, thought, and consciousness.

attention: A factor of the mind that purposely engages consciousness to focus on a particular object. One of the five interlinked factors of perception.

bhikkhu: A fully ordained monk. A member of the Buddha's Sangha, or community of followers.

cessation: Ending. It is the Buddha's third noble truth, the promise that suffering has an end. Cessation with no further rebirths is nibbana, liberation, freedom from suffering.

contact: A factor that arises in the mind from the meeting of a sense organ, an appropriate sensory object, and consciousness, for example, the ear, a bird singing, and consciousness. One of the five interlinked mental factors of perception.

delusion: The confused belief in a permanently existing self or soul. We believe that there must be something real and permanent called I or me that is identical with the body and mind or within the body and mind.

dependent origination: Anything that depends for its existence on impermanent and ever-changing causes and conditions. All such things arise, remain for a time, and then disappear.

dhamma (when lowercased): Phenomena. Also the true nature of phenomena, as taught by the Buddha—his profound insight that all conditioned phenomena are impermanent, suffering, and selfless.

Dhamma (capitalized): The teachings of the Buddha.

disenchantment: The mental attitude of disinterest and nonattachment that arises when we recognize the impermanent, suffering, and selfless nature of all conditioned things.

dispassion: The opposite of attachment. One of ten special perceptions that arise as a result of mindfulness meditation. Mindful that everything that arises as a result of causes and conditions is impermanent, unsatisfactory, and selfless, you experience dispassion and abandon the belief that attachment to anything in this world can make you permanently happy.

enlightenment: Full and complete liberation from suffering. By attaining enlightenment, the Buddha and arahants have attained cessation. Having eliminated the fetters that bind someone to the cycle of births and deaths, they will not take rebirth in any form anywhere.

equanimity: A mental state that is perfectly peaceful and balanced, experiencing neither desire nor aversion.

feeling: A factor of the mind that categorizes or judges what is being perceived as pleasant, unpleasant, or neither pleasant nor unpleasant. One of the five interlinked mental factors of perception.

fetter: The ten deep-rooted habits of the unenlightened mind that bind us to one unsatisfactory life after another: belief in a permanent self, skeptical doubt, clinging to rituals, sensory craving, hatred, craving for fine material existence, craving for immaterial existence, conceit, restlessness, and ignorance.

five aggregates: The traditional constituents of the body and mind: form, feeling, perception, thought, and consciousness. Form refers to every material thing that the senses can perceive, including the various parts of the body. The other four include all experiences of the mind.

four foundations of mindfulness: Moment-to-moment awareness of the body, feelings, thoughts, and dhamma or phenomena.

Four Noble Truths: The Buddha's first essential teaching, delivered at the Deer Park near Varanasi after he achieved enlightenment: (1) the truth of suffering; (2) the truth of the cause of suffering—craving; (3) the truth of cessation—the end of suffering; and (4) the noble eight-fold path—the step-by-step method to ending suffering.

four tetrads: The sixteen meditation topics in the tenth perception of the Girimananda Sutta can be divided into four groups of four, each group corresponding to one of the Four Foundations of Mindfulness.

hindrance: Negative tendencies that obstruct our spiritual progress and interfere with our ability to concentrate. They include sense desire, ill will, sloth and torpor, restlessness and worry, and skeptical doubt. Concentration meditation suppresses the hindrances temporarily, but only the jhana states of concentrated meditation can eliminate them.

insight meditation: Also called vipassana or mindfulness meditation. Focused awareness that helps us gain insight into the nature of the body, feelings, thoughts, and phenomena.

jhana: The stages of deep concentration meditation that take meditators beyond ordinary mindfulness into a series of deeply tranquil, harmonious, and powerful states.

kamma: The universal principle of cause and effect. Our countless actions of body, speech, and mind are causes. Our present life and everything that happens to us are the effects that arise from the causes we created in this life or previous lives. In general, good actions lead to good results and bad actions to bad results.

liberation: Complete freedom from suffering. Nibbana. The state of being free from the cycle of repeated births and deaths in samsara propelled by kamma and craving.

mental factor: An impermanent aspect of mental functioning, such as contact, feeling, attention, perception, energy, and mindfulness.

mental formation: Any impermanent thought or idea, such as a memory, emotion, or concept. A mind object that can be perceived by consciousness.

mindfulness: Clear moment-to-moment awareness of what is happening as it happens.

nibbana: The goal of the path—liberation, the extinction of delusion, freedom from the life-after-life cycle of births and deaths. In some Buddhist traditions, "nirvana."

Noble Eightfold Path: The Buddha's fourth noble truth, eight steps to freedom from suffering: skillful understanding, skillful thinking, skillful speech, skillful action, skillful livelihood, skillful effort, skillful mindfulness, and skillful concentration.

perception: A mental factor that arises as a result of the meeting between a sense organ, a sensory object, consciousness, contact, attention, and feeling.

samatha: Concentration meditation. Sometimes translated as "calm abiding." This peaceful, one-pointed mind suppresses the hindrances and makes the mind calm, peaceful, and luminous.

samsara: The life-after-life cycle of birth, illness, aging, and death characterized by suffering.

selflessness: The Buddha's insight that no person has a permanent self or soul and that nothing that exists has an unchanging core. Also called emptiness.

seven factors of enlightenment: Bojjhangas, in Pali: mindfulness, investigation, energy, joy, tranquility, concentration, and equanimity.

The word comes from *bodhi*, which means "enlightenment," and *anga*, which means limb.

signlessness: The state of mind that realizes that everything that exists is impermanent and that it fades away without leaving behind any sign or trace of its existence.

sutta: Buddhist scripture, especially a narrative or discourse traditionally considered to be delivered by the Buddha or one of his well-known disciples.

wishlessness: The state of mind that recognizes that since the desire or wish for any conditioned thing leads only to frustration and suffering, wishing for anything is meaningless.

vipassana: Insight, especially into the true nature of the self and of phenomena. The realization that everything that is conditioned is impermanent, suffering, and selfless.

INDEX

Page numbers followed by "(2)" or "(3)" indicate two or three references.

ABOUT THE AUTHOR

 BHANTE HENEPOLA GUNARATANA was ordained as a Buddhist monk at the age of twelve in Malandeniya, Sri Lanka. He's the author of *Mindfulness in Plain English*, *Eight Mindful Steps to Happiness*, and several more books—including his autobiography, *Journey to Mindfulness*. He travels and teaches throughout the world, and currently lives at Bhavana Society Forest Monastery in West Virginia.

More Books by Bhante Gunaratana
from Wisdom Publications

Mindfulness in Plain English

"A masterpiece. I cannot recommend it highly enough."
—Jon Kabat-Zinn, author of *Wherever You Go, There You Are*

The Four Foundations of Mindfulness in Plain English

"Bhante G's calming tone will put even the newest
Dharma practitioner at ease."
—*Tricycle*

Journey to Mindfulness
The Autobiography of Bhante G.

"Like the stories of the wisest and kindest of grandfathers.
A joy to read."
—Sylvia Boorstein, author of *It's Easier Than You Think*

Beyond Mindfulness in Plain English
An Introductory Guide to Deeper States of Meditation

"Succinct and clear, this book provides the reader with valuable
tools to further their practice and to train the mind."
—Sharon Salzberg, cofounder of the Insight Meditation Society

About Wisdom Publications

Wisdom Publications is the leading publisher of classic and contemporary Buddhist books and practical works on mindfulness. To learn more about us or to explore our other books, please visit our website at wisdomexperience.org or contact us at the address below.

Wisdom Publications
199 Elm Street
Somerville, MA 02144 USA

We are a 501(c)(3) organization, and donations in support of our mission are tax deductible.

Wisdom Publications is affiliated with the Foundation for the Preservation of the Mahayana Tradition (FPMT).